# What They Said About THE IBM XT CLONE BUYER'S GUIDE

"I highly recommend it to anyone contemplating getting a computer...." Jerry Pournelle, **BYTE MAGAZINE**

"It outlines everything you need to know about piecing together your own clone or what to look for when buying an assembled clone." John C. Dvorak, **SAN FRANCISCO EXAMINER**

"A useful resource for those thinking about buying a PC clone." Lawrence Magid, **LOS ANGELES TIMES**

"You should get this book before you buy any computer." Art Kleiner, **WHOLE EARTH REVIEW**

"It contains good, hard information presented in a breezy, easy-to-read style that novices will delight in." **TEXAS COMPUTER MARKET**

"Author, Edwin Rutsch, provides a well-written overview of the IBM family of personal computers. Anyone new to the computer arena will be served well by his description of the IBM PC's." Morgan D'Arcy, **FOGLIGHT**

"....Edwin Rutsch has performed a valuable service to the microcomputer consumer...." **NORTH TEXAS PC USER GROUP**

"Thank you for writing such a concise and easily understandable book on PC clones. Thanks to you I was able to go to several stores, speak with some authority on the merits of the computers I was shown, discover that some stores had salespeople who knew less than I, and in the end, make what I felt was a good choice." Kate Freeman, Los Angeles, California.

# IBM XT CLONE

## Buyer's Guide and Handbook

## Edwin Rutsch

The
Boston
Computer
Society

One Center Plaza

Boston,

Massachusetts

02108

7/89

**Technical Researchers**
**Ian Hughes**
**Jean-Pierre Chelouche**

## Modular Information Systems

☞ **First Edition, October 1988**

The
Boston
Computer
Society

One Center Plaza

Boston,

Massachusetts

02108

7/89

**Published by;**

**Modular Information Systems**
431 Ashbury Street
San Francisco, California 94117
(415) 552-8648   BBS (415) 552-9070

**Notice of Liability**
While every effort for accuracy is made, the information in this book is
distributed on an "as is" basis, without warranty. Neither the Author nor
Modular Information Systems shall have any liability to any person or
entity with respect to any liability, loss, or damage caused directly or indirectly by information contained in this book.

IBM XT is a registered trademark of International Business Machines.
Many of the designations used by manufacturers and sellers to distin-
guish their products are claimed as trademarks. When those designations appear in this book, and MIS was aware of a trademark claim, the
designations have been printed in bold or bold italics.

Printed and bound in the United States of America

Distributed to the book trade by **Publishers Group West**  415/658-3453

ISBN 0-939325-18-7

# Table of Contents

# TABLE OF ILLUSTRATIONS

*xv*

# List of Tables

# About the Author

Edwin Rutsch lives in San Francisco, California and heads a microcomputer consulting and book publishing firm. He also holds seminars on the purchasing and using of computers.

Mr. Rutsch has been in the computer field since the inception of the clone market. He has worked with clones as a dealer, a consultant, an organizer (founding a national computer users group), and as a lecturer. He is also author of the IBM AT CLONE BUYER'S GUIDE AND HANDBOOK as well as the 386 COMPUTER BUYER'S GUIDE AND HANDBOOK. He is presently working on his next book, the PS/2 CLONE BUYER'S GUIDE AND HANDBOOK.

Mr. Rutsch has studied and traveled abroad extensively. He graduated in 1984 from the University of Texas with a degree in Economics.

# About the Technical Editor

Ian Hughes is a native of Pennsylvania who came to California in 1982. A graduate of the Pennsylvania State University, he now lives in San Francisco, CA where he works as a consultant in computers, computer typesetting, telecommunications and desktop publishing. He has contributed to numerous computer books and written several technical manuals. Mr. Hughes has been involved in computers and computer book publishing since 1983. He is presently working on a complete beginners guide to computers.

# About the Technical Researcher

Jean-Pierre Chelouche, a native of Grenoble, France, now lives in Alameda, California, and has been in America since 1972. He is the head of **Powerlight Systems**, a consulting firm specializing in IBM compatible desktop computer systems. Installation of 286 and 386 systems represents the bulk of his activity. Mr. Chelouche also conducts seminars and lectures on computer hardware assembly. Mr. Chelouche graduated from the University of Grenoble in 1964 with a degree in electrical engineering. He followed this up with a second degree in 1966 from the Gold Fachschule in Zurich, Switzerland.

# Acknowledgements

*Special thanks to fellow PC Clone User Group members for their assistance*

Writing and publishing a book is an unbelievably complicated and time-consuming task and typically involves a lot more than the efforts of the so-called writer. The many support people involved usually get little recognition for their very large and important contributions. Here, I have chosen to break the traditional format of an acknowledgment page to give several of these hard working people a line of their own and to give a little boost to their companies.

With all my heart I wish to thank the following people for their efforts.

Ian Hughes, Technical Researcher and Ventura Guru, (415) 931-3765, for his research, editing and assistance with the book's layout and typesetting with the Ventura desktop publishing program.....as well as for humorous inspiration.

Jean-Pierre Chelouche, of **Powerlight Systems**, (415) 523-1139, for his research and editing of technical information.

Catherine Curtis, of **Curtis Communications**, (414) 626-3549, for her expertise at the marketing analysis and promotion of this book.

George Omura, of **Omura Illustrations**, (415) 523-1113, for the *AutoCad*-generated computer assembly illustrations in chapter 7 & 8.

Joseph Grossman, of **Enabling Technologies Inc.**, (312) 427-0386, for the *Pro3D*-generated computer drawings which occur on each chapter page throughout the book.

Abbas Merchant, for his database and accounting expertise and assistance with *Dbase*.

Ed Connors, (415) 528-8180, for the *AutoCad*-generated illustrations on pages 45, 184, 187, 202, and 220.

Mike Andrews, (408) 379-5788, for the cover design.

Ralph Portillo, of Portillo-Kester Photography, (415) 285-2455, for the cover photography.

Thanks to the following members of the PC Clone Clone User Group of San Francisco, who "Beta Tested" this book:  Barbara Thomason, Claude Fitzgerald, George Hayes, Peter Graf, Steve Dougherty, Norm Garrick, Pam Mitchell, Dorothy Bowhall,  Bob Christenberry, Robert Dupruy, Bill Copenhaven, Virgil Allison, Stan James, and Dana Smith.

Also, I would like to make very special thanks to my mother and father, Jenny and Gerhard Rutsch, for their extraordinary support during the long and tedious task of developing and writing this book.

# Production Note

I wish to thank the many companies who generously supplied their products for me to use and review.

The manuscript for this book was written using *WordPerfect*, a word processing program by the **WordPerfect Corporation** of Orem, Utah. The manuscript and page formatting was done with *Ventura Publisher 1.1*, a desktop-publishing program from the **Xerox Corporation**. The telecommunications involved in producing this book was accomplished by use of *Carbon Copy*, a software program by **Meridian Technology** of Newport Beach, California. Camera-ready copy was produced on a *LaserJet* laser printer which is manufactured by **Hewlett-Packard.**

The book was written and produced on an *Everex 386* from **Everex Systems, Inc**, of Fremont, California. The monitor used was a *Wyse 700* manufactured by **Wyse Technologies** of San Jose, California. The hard disk used was a 44-megabyte *Miniscribe 6053* manufactured by **MiniScribe Corporation** of Longmont, Colorado.

The three-dimensional rotating computer drawings at the beginning of each chapter were made with a software package called *Pro3D* from the **Enabling Technology Inc.** of Chicago, Illinois. The illustrations in chapter 7 and 8 were created by the use of *AutoCad,* a computer aided-design program from the **Autodesk Company** of Sausalito, California.

The cartoons are of old, public-domain Victorian-era engravings. Captions are courtesy of Edwin and Ian and too much coffee late at night.

The printing is by **McNaughton and Gunn Inc.** of Ann Arbor, Michigan.

*Author and technical editor "interfacing" about illustration captions*

# Introduction

Figure i.1    *Buying a new computer can be a joyous event*

A tremendous number of companies have introduced very low cost IBM XT type computers onto the market. The consumer who is interested in buying such a machine, very likely wants to know what is the best price, quality, and performance available. For many (perhaps even most) consumers, the job of selecting a computer can become a sizable research project. One can spend days, sometimes months, making sense out of the voluminous array of information. For some people all this can be a bit straining.

This guide is intended to assist you in acquiring the best computer for your needs and pocketbook while expending the least amount of time and effort in the search. It covers many of the different types of lower cost computers now on the market. The conclusion is that an XT clone is now the best deal for the budget conscious buyer.

This book also serves as a **reference manual** so that you can get the most from your XT clone once purchased. This is accomplished through the tutorial format of the handbook sections that are primarily in the latter half of the book. The handbook chapters familiarize you with your computer's parts and capabilities. There is also a glossary at the back of this book to especially aid the beginner.

I have designed this book in such a manner that the reader can pick and choose what is appropriate for his or her interest at any given moment. I felt that a format with simple to-the-point explanations would more likely meet the needs of the reader than taking a high-tech approach that only the computer sophisticate could or would read.

I have started this book with a chapter showing a historical overview of the microcomputer's development. While not being immediately helpful in making your purchase of an XT clone, this chapter should help in the long run, in that it makes for a clearer perspective of where the computer industry has been and the direction it is headed.

The second chapter further introduces the task of purchasing a computer by discussing some basic differences between the various generations of computers.

For the well-informed "computer person," perhaps it is more reasonable that you skip to Chapter Three, or whatever chapter catches your interest in the table of contents. I have tried to address your needs as well as those who are less experienced with computers.

In the book's organization, I have opened each chapter in a "reader-friendly" fashion, allowing it to progress into more sophisticated and technical talk towards the end. If, for some of you, everything in this book is not understood, please don't feel that you can't buy, own and operate a computer. It simply isn't so. Computers are not as complicated as one might be lead to think.

The steps and parts used in assembling an XT clone are explained in Chapter Seven so that anyone, with even the smallest amount of experience in mechanical matters can assemble his or her own clone. Chapters Six and Seven explain how to expand your computer's capabilities and Chapter Eight makes it possible for you to do your own troubleshooting.

Because of the rapidly advancing technology in the personal computer field, a buyer's guide and handbook needs frequent revisions. For this reason I have produced this book using the latest desktop

Figure i.2     Ian, Jean-Pierre, Catherine, and Edwin checking the latest edition of the
IBM XT CLONE BUYER'S GUIDE AND HANDBOOK

publishing techniques. This allows me to produce an updated version with every new printing so that you will have the latest up-to-date information.

In the back of the book is a questionnaire for your feedback on this book. If you are so inclined, fill it out and send it in. I look forward to hearing from you.

Enjoy.

*Edwin Rutsch*

Edwin Rutsch
San Francisco, California

# Section I

# Buyer's Guide

# CHAPTER 1

# OVERVIEW OF THE PERSONAL COMPUTER'S DEVELOPMENT

# Chapter Focus

Chapter one is written especially for the person who does not have a basic understanding of personal computers.  The chapter has two functions:

1. To give the reader a short history of the personal computer over the last decade and

2. To introduce and explain some typical terms and ideas that will be helpful in understanding the task of buying and using a personal computer. The format of this chapter is periodically supplemented by special explanations in framed boxes  for the purpose of clarifying certain important concepts.

There are some words in this chapter which are italicized; this is a flagging method to let the reader know that this word, which is undefined in the text, can be found in the glossary.

*Figure 1.1*   Getting an overview can be an adventure

\* \* \* \* \*

IN NO OTHER field do standards change and companies rise and fall as quickly as they do in the computer industry. A particular generation of computers comes on the scene and seemingly overnight becomes obsolete as another generation is born. Each computer company struggles to beat out the competition, and the end result is that there are continuously more computers to choose from.  In the end, the task of keeping track of the latest developments seems to be impossible. With proper knowledge you can, however, resolve the dilemmas which face you as a computer buyer. You can make an intelligent selection of an entire computer or simply select computer expansion parts from the dizzying array of choices.  The first step in becoming an informed shopper is to have an overview of the major developments in the microcomputer industry.

# In the Beginning

The personal computer started coming of age in the late 1970's with the first so-called "microcomputers." This term was chosen in order to emphasize the small, desk-top size of this new computer. Before the microcomputer's arrival, the computer industry had consisted of large and very expensive machines that were used mostly by large companies, the rich, and the powerful...those who could afford such costly items. Oddly enough, the innovative concept of the "personal" computer was not introduced by the large standard-setting companies such as IBM. Instead, it was developed and introduced instead by relatively unknown entrepreneurial companies such as Apple, Morrow, Osborne, Kaypro, and North Star (to name but a few).

In the beginning of the microcomputers' evolution, there were many different personal computers available. However, only two particular types caught on well with consumers. These two microcomputers were the Apple II series and CP/M-based computers. They were distinctly different in that their hardware (the physical parts of a machine) worked with entirely different "operating systems."

> The operating system is a software program which controls the computer hardware. There are many types of operating systems. Some examples are *"CP/M," "Apple-DOS,"* "MS-DOS," "OS/2," and *"UNIX."* The operating system gives you complete control over what your computer is basically capable of doing and gives you control over how it does it. The operating system program is typically stored on a *"floppy disk"* or on *a "hard disk."*

One of the basic tasks of the operating system program is to allow the computer to run other programs which are more task-specific in design. These are called "application programs" or software packages. Three examples of typical software packages that are available are those designed for *word processing*, *database management*, and *spreadsheet tasks*. There are literally thousands of application programs available on the market, but all are written to work in conjunction with some specific operating system; they cannot be made to work alone. The software must have compatibility with the particular operating system that the computer is using in order to work correctly.

*Figure 1.2*    Early computers did not need an operating system

## Enter the Apple II-Series

The Apple Company's "Apple II-series" microcomputers came onto the computer market with rapid and extraordinary success. Its exclusive operating system seemed to do its job very adequately, while the computer owed much of its success to simply being one of the first viable microcomputers on the market. Also important in its success was the hardware design of partially "open architecture." This feature strongly increased the usefulness and popularity of the Apple II's.

> "Open architecture" is a very handy and practical idea. What it means is that the machine is designed so that the user can open it up and exchange or add parts for the purpose of expanding the computer's capabilities.
>
> There are varying degrees of open architecture. The most simple and typical modification is accomplished by adding what is called "expansion boards". The more "open" a computer, the more exchanging or adding that can be done. Some computers are even designed so all of their parts can be changed in some way for the purpose of expanding the computers' capabilities.

This open architecture concept allowed independent parts makers to design and produce replacement and add-on parts; this soon lead to intense competition among these companies to produce parts with greater and greater capabilities. The user directly benefited because soon there were so many parts available with which to expand the computer.

## The CP/M-Based Computer

The so-called "CP/M" (Control Program/Monitor) operating system, designed by Gary Kildall, was being used by many of the other entrepreneurial computer manufacturing companies. For a fee, Mr. Kildall licensed computer manufacturers to use his CP/M operating system. Such companies as Morrow, Osborne, and Kaypro, among others, chose to use the CP/M operating system for their versions of personal computers.

Although computers that were based on the CP/M operating system became very popular on the market, their popularity was not with the general public (as was the case with Apple) but with the business world. Small businesses had become increasingly interested in the relatively inexpensive microcomputers and were especially drawn to the CP/M based computers.

## Enter the IBM PC

Thus, Apple-II computers and the CP/M based computers became the standard for the microcomputer industry. They maintained their strong positions until the early 1980's and probably would have continued as the standard much longer if it hadn't been for the entrance of IBM into the personal computer market.

When IBM decided to enter the microcomputer market, they were still dubious of its potential. They speculated that the personal computer market would be small at best and as a result, they did not put much effort into the development of such a product. They formed a small division in Boca Raton, Florida, to handle this relatively minor project, instructing the project director to get a personal computer into the marketplace quickly.

In August 1981, IBM (the world's largest computer manufacturer) finally introduced its own microcomputer.

IBM's version of the personal computer did not use either of the previous operating systems. IBM had asked a company called Microsoft to produce for them a new operating system which would work with their entry into the microcomputer market.

Microsoft accepted the design contract and successfully produced an operating system for IBM. IBM made a few small changes and then gave it an IBM name. They called it "PC-DOS," which stood for "Personal Computer-Disk Operating System." Meanwhile, Microsoft kept the right to sell, under their own name, the program that they had originally designed. Microsoft called it "MS-DOS" (the letters stood for Microsoft-Disk Operating System). MS-DOS became a very successful product for Microsoft and, in fact, ultimately became the standard operating system for the personal computer market.

IBM called their microcomputer the "IBM PC," which simply meant the IBM Personal Computer. Actually, as it turned out, the IBM PC was not such a creative breakthrough for the market as IBM made it seem. Its operating system, for example, had been designed by Microsoft to include many of the features that were found in the CP/M operating system. IBM also borrowed the idea of open architecture from the Apple II series.

IBM had been known for making and controlling virtually all aspects of their products, however, with their entrance into the microcomputer field, they broke with this tradition. They manufactured the PC with *off-the-shelf components* (those made by other manufacturers). The reason IBM did this was to save time in getting a personal computer out onto the market. By using other companies' ideas and components, the development process speeded up dramatically. However, it also meant that IBM would have little to patent or copyright.

Within a year and a half, the IBM PC had established itself as the leader in the field of personal computers. Business users saw it as a more viable product than what had come before. As the IBM PC became the de facto microcomputer standard for the business community, CP/M-based computers rapidly lost ground.

The Apple II-series, however, continued to hold its ground in the market by being marketed more toward educational and home use. Apple had, in fact, placed computers (as gifts or near-gifts) in many schools across the nation. This helped establish Apple a solid place in the market, at least for the time being.

*Figure 1.3*    IBM used off-the-shelf components when they made the PC

## Enter the IBM XT

In March of 1983, IBM introduced its second microcomputer, the IBM XT. IBM took the letters "XT" from the center of the word "extra". This emphasis on the notion of "eXTra" was intended to point out that this particular microcomputer had greater expansion capabilities over its predecessor. The IBM PC was designed with only five expansion slots whereas the IBM XT had eight. Another extra was that of power, the PC had a meager 63 watt power supply versus 135 watts for the XT.

## "Compatible" Manufacturers Follow IBM

After the giant, standard-setting IBM established a firm foothold in the microcomputer market, most of the other personal computer manufacturers saw the writing on the wall. They could either adopt the IBM standard or face going out of business since most software packages being produced were being designed for the MS-DOS Operating System.

In response, many companies began to develop and sell computers that were software "compatible" with IBM's PC and XT. This ability to run the same software was made possible by the fact that they also used MS-DOS. These machines simply became known as "compatibles".

> Examples of companies that make compatibles are AT&T, Compaq, Epson, Leading Edge, Kaypro, and Tandy.

# Timeline of the Personal

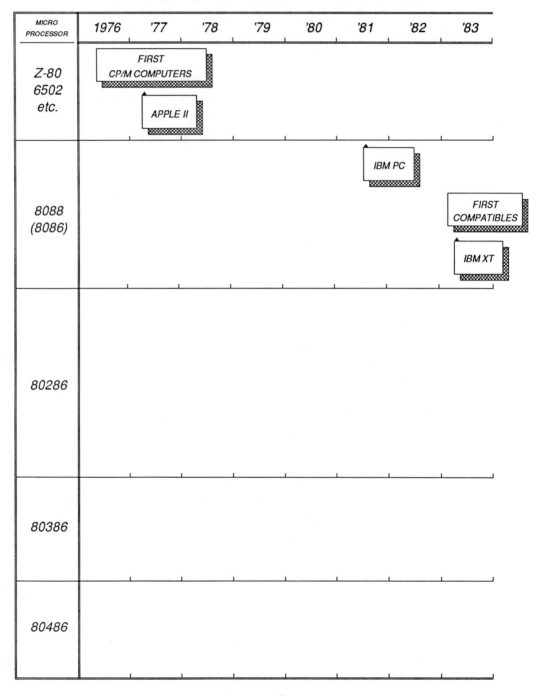

| MICRO PROCESSOR | 1976 | '77 | '78 | '79 | '80 | '81 | '82 | '83 |
|---|---|---|---|---|---|---|---|---|

**Z-80 6502 etc.**
FIRST CP/M COMPUTERS
APPLE II

**8088 (8086)**
IBM PC
FIRST COMPATIBLES
IBM XT

**80286**

**80386**

**80486**

# Computers Development

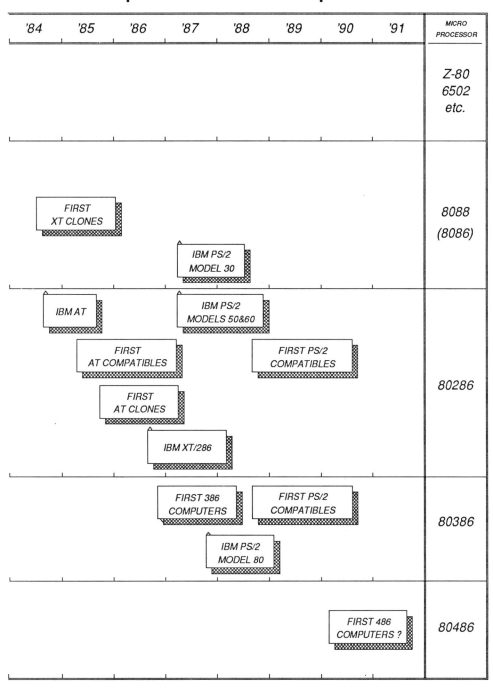

It is important to note that these compatibles, while able to use most of the software programs written for the IBM personal computers, are not so compatible when it comes to hardware. Some parts of the IBM PC and XT hardware can be used in these compatibles and some cannot. It varies within each brand as to how many parts in the machine are interchangeable.

*Figure 1.4*   The computer business is becoming increasingly competitive

# Enter the "Parts Makers"

Within a relatively short period, the IBM XTs (as well as some of the compatibles) had become very successful on the market. The easy ability to expand the capability of these machines created a huge demand for expansion products. Companies in the United States and Asia quickly moved to supply the many owners of such machines with the expansion boards that they so eagerly wanted. These companies were soon making "add-on parts" that added new and better features to the computer (such parts as: *modems, floppy disk drives, monitors, multiple input/output cards, memory boards*, and so on).

Soon after the add-ons for PCs, XTs, and compatibles were successfully brought onto the market, parts makers started bringing out a large line of replacement parts, particularly those used in the IBM XT. Before long, the parts companies had added to their low-cost list virtually all the parts that were to be found in the IBM XT. These parts, mostly made in Taiwan, were of generally good quality and sold at less than half the price of IBM parts.

# Enter the IBM XT Clone

Since all the add-on parts for the IBM XT were almost identical and readily available, it was only a matter of time before the parts manufacturers (and other companies too) were assembling the parts into whole completed computers. These machines were copies of the original IBM XT computer to the point where even the physical dimensions and looks were the same. These particular computers became known as "XT clones."

All parts of an XT clone were made to be completely interchangeable with all parts (inside and out) of its IBM counterpart.
If IBM produced what the world would call a quality computer
by producing the IBM XT, then the same could have been said
about the IBM XT clones since they were faithful replicas.

The IBM XT clones, which first appeared in early 1985,
turned out to be extremely popular. They came primarily from
Asian manufacturers who were doing what they were (and still
are) famous for, that is, the mass production of low cost and relatively high quality electronic products. A few of the parts for
XT clones were being manufactured in the United States. Typically, what would happen is that American manufacturers would
come up with a new add-on feature for IBM's open-architecture
computers and, within a year or two, Asian manufacturers
(primarily Taiwanese) would begin producing a low-cost replica
of that part.

XT clones in general, have now grown to such a degree of
popularity that they dominate computer shows, advertising space
in most computer publications, the computer mail order business
as well as sales at an increasing number of computer stores.

# Evolution into the Next Generation

While the clone makers were busy manufacturing XT clones, IBM was not just sitting idly by. IBM's designers were busily working on their next model, a model which would usher in a new "generation."

The word "generation," in this context, is actually a computer-industry term that has a very specific meaning regarding computers. It does not necessarily refer to a company's "next-model-out" on the market. A so-called "new generation" occurs only when a manufacturer brings out a computer model that is based on a new type of "central processing unit" (CPU or sometimes also referred to as a "microprocessor"). Several manufacturers then, can and do have different models which are all based on that same microprocessor.

This central processing unit is only one of many types of chips used by the computer industry. A computer chip, of course, is basically a small complex circuit which is etched onto a tiny silicon wafer no bigger than a dime. The CPU is the most important chip in a computer. It is, in a sense, the computer's "brain" and determines the nature as well as the capability of the particular computer it resides in.

## Enter the IBM "AT" Generation

In August of 1984, IBM took the wraps off its second microcomputer generation. They called it the IBM "AT," which stood for "Advanced Technology." It was based on a newly developed central processing unit which was manufactured by the Intel Corporation of Santa Clara, California. Intel called it the "80286" chip (also referred to as simply the "286").

The IBM PC and XT were also based on an Intel chip, the "8088." The 80286, which followed the 8088, represented a quantum leap in the evolution of the microprocessor. It enabled companies to manufacture more powerful and more capable computers. This IBM AT, with its new 80286 CPU, was physically larger than the XT computer. The AT was enthusiastically received by business and professional users who were eager for more power and greater speed. It also had several other features that were especially advantageous to this particular group of users.

One advantage that attracted business/professional people to the IBM AT was that it was *"downward compatible"* with the PC and XT. What this meant was that much of the previously written software and existing add-on hardware could be used with little or no trouble in the AT. This meant that offices already equipped with the previous generation of IBM microcomputers had no problem bringing in ATs to add with existing office equipment. Another advantage was that the IBM AT was not only faster than its predecessor but it came with more storage capabilities.

Open architecture was a continued concept in IBM's newest personal computer. This meant the AT computer could also be copied by the competition.

## The IBM AT Compatibles

Approximately six months after the original IBM AT was released, there were already some compatibles available from Kaypro, Compaq, Sperry, and ITT. Clearly, the competition was hot on IBM's polished heels. Just as had been the case with the previous generation, these compatibles were software compatible with the IBM AT. Also the hardware was again only partially the same.

## Enter the IBM AT Clones

Clone manufacturers were not very far behind IBM and the compatible manufacturers in getting an AT clone onto the market. The companies that were making clones reproduced a reasonable quality replica of an IBM original with total hardware interchangeability for less than half the price.

## The Clone Makers Bring Out a "Baby AT"

Shortly after the clone makers brought out their version of IBM's AT, they went one step further; they introduced a modified version of an IBM machine. This new model functioned the same as the IBM AT, but was the size of the smaller XT. The clone makers were able to manufacture this smaller AT clone because they had used a combined set of chips which took up less room inside the computer, making the finished product smaller.

The clone makers weren't sure what to call this smaller computer. It wasn't exactly a clone, since IBM had not brought one out yet. The industry tried several names: "Baby AT," "Baby 286," "Mini AT," and "Mini 286" (the name that seems to have stuck has been the Baby AT).

The acceptance of the Baby AT's was only moderate in the beginning, the reason being that some people simply preferred the bigger and more impressive AT case. Perhaps, their thinking was nothing more than psychological – the bigger the size, the greater the power, the greater the status.

## Next Comes the IBM "XT286"

In September of 1986, IBM brought out a second model which was based on the Intel 80286 chip. The actual physical size was the same as the IBM XT and the clone makers Baby AT, yet fundamentally this computer had the same features as the big IBM AT. This machine did not fare well. It was slower than the IBM AT and yet was priced at almost the same price as the original AT.

IBM did not call this computer a Baby AT. They called it the IBM XT286. This however, was both misleading and confusing since it made the prospective buyer think that it was both an XT (based on the 8088 chip) and a 286-based computer. It was not both, it was actually only a 286-based machine that was fitted into an XT chassis – hence, the name XT286. For all practical purposes it can definitely fit in the category of Baby ATs.

## The Birth of the "80386" Generation: Via the Clone and Compatible Makers

Following the 80286 chip, the Intel Corporation released to the general market a new, more powerful microprocessor chip, the 80386...commonly called the "386." This was another leap forward in CPU technology. Much to the surprise of the computer industry, clever clone and compatible makers brought out the new 386 generation of computers before IBM. They were able to get them developed and onto the market as early as the end of 1986.

These new, powerful, personal computers based on the 80386 chip hold the promise of eventually placing the power of mainframe computers within the reach of any serious microcomputer users. They also will open the door to the availability of sophisticated *"artificial intelligence" (AI)* programs.

*Figure 1.5*    An early mainframe

## IBM's 386 Model and a Whole Lot More

The clone and compatible makers performed quite a coup in bringing their 386 out before IBM had brought out theirs. However, IBM soon followed with a coup of their own. In the spring of 1987, IBM announced a whole new line of microcomputers that would replace all their present line.

The new line would be a general departure from the previous hardware standard that they themselves had created. IBM called their new line of microcomputers the "Personal Systems/2 Series" (PS/2 for short). Three models in the line were to come out immediately, the PS/2 Model 30, the PS/2 Model 50, and the PS/2 Model 60. In the fall they would bring out their model that was to be based on the Intel 386 chip, the PS/2 Model 80.

With the new line there were definite changes. It was as if IBM were trying to go back and correct some of their mistakes which had allowed the cloners to copy their models. This time there were no off-the-shelf components. The computers used entirely new parts and all were copyrighted by IBM. For the more powerful computers in the line (the PS/2 Model 50 and above), IBM had included a different and improved *"bus"* structure. This new structure meant that they were introducing a new hardware standard. The thousands of previously-designed expansion boards could not be used in any of IBM's new line of computers that used the Micro Channel.

## The Future 80486 Generation

The development of new CPU computer chips by Intel is continuing at a rapid rate. The 80486 is now on the drawing board and computers which will be based on this chip could be available by 1990. Intel has stated that this chip will continue to be downward compatible with previous chips. What this chip will mean to the personal computer industry is not yet known, but in all likelihood it will have great impact and be another leap forward in the development of the personal computer.

*Figure 1.6*    Intel employees are now working on the 80486 chip

# Non Intel-Based Computers

This chapter has presented an overview of the history of the personal computer and has focused on computers that are based on Intel's central processing units.  However, it should also be mentioned that there are other companies that design and manufacture CPUs.  There is in fact a second CPU standard in the microcomputer industry.  It is the 68000 series, which is manufactured by Motorola of Phoenix, Arizona.

Several very popular computers are based on the Motorola CPUs.  Some examples are the Apple Macintosh, the  Atari ST, and the Commodore Amiga.

The computers which are using the Motorola microprocessor have outstanding graphic capabilities, while those using Intel's are strong in business applications, such as word processing, databases, and spreadsheets.  The Intel-based computers are however, catching up in the field of graphics.

The computer companies that use Motorola CPUs have designed their own independent operating systems.  This makes their computers completely incompatible with all other computers that are on the market, even others that use the same Motorola CPU.  This is a rather large penalty in that a relatively small selection  of software available for these computers.  The user does not have the choice of thousands of software packages to choose from as they do with computers using the Intel CPU.

# IBM PS/2 Clones and Compatibles

In April 1988, both Tandy and Dell Computers announced computers compatible with IBM's 286 and 386-based PS/2 computers. There were also several other computer manufacturers in this country as well as the Far East which expressed their determination to come out with PS/2 compatible computers by the end of 1988. These computers represent the beginning of a new hardware standard which many computer analysts predict will become the dominant standard in a few years. IBM has however, protected its new computers with patents which has made it difficult for the compatible and clone makers to make knockoffs of the PS/2 line as they did with the XT and AT.

# The Future of the Microcomputer

There are many questions that have arisen due to IBM's latest maneuvers in the microcomputer market. Will IBM be able to protect its turf with the new hardware standard? Will the nimble competition create clones and steal away some or all of IBM's new market as they have previously done? Will computer buyers purchase these computers in a big way? If you, as a consumer, purchase a computer from among the old standard, will you be left in the dust of technological obsolescence?

These and many more questions affecting the future are now on the minds of the industry analysts, computer users, and especially computer buyers. Many of these questions will be addressed in the following chapters.

# CHAPTER 2

# IS AN XT CLONE FOR YOU?

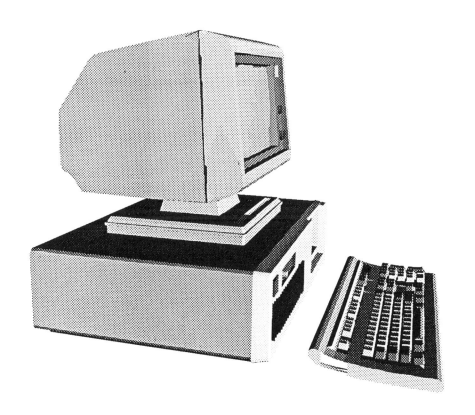

# Chapter Focus

This chapter helps clarify the differences in features and capabilities between the generations of computers that are based on the Intel 8088, 80286, and 80386 microprocessors. It will help you decide how powerful a machine you need. It may be that an XT clone is simply not enough machine for your needs.

This chapter is divided into two parts. The first part describes, in easy-to-understand terms, the advantages and disadvantages of each generation of computer. This is followed in the second part by a more technical comparison of the capabilities of each generation.

*Figure 2.1*    Deciding which generation of computer to purchase takes some thought

\* \* \* \* \*

AS MENTIONED in the previous chapter, there are presently three generations of computers for you to choose from if you are going with the IBM standard.  They are the computers which use one of the three Intel made microprocessors.  The most basic difference between the three generations of computers is simply that each is based on a different microprocessor and therefore carries different capabilities.  The purpose of this chapter is to help you choose the correct generation of computer for your needs and pocketbook.

If you are already convinced that you need an 8088-based computer, the comparisons in this chapter will still be of benefit by helping you to better understand the capabilities of this machine.

The following are some helpful points to remember as you read further:

**8088** refers to both the microprocessor and to all the computers based on the Intel 8088 chip. This term includes such computers as the IBM PC, XT, XT clones, and compatibles. The **8086** chips are functionally identical to the 8088 chip and are the central processing units on which some compatibles as well as the IBM Personal System/2 Models 25 and 30 are based. (Generally, when the 8088 chip is discussed, the 8086 is meant as well.)

**80286** (or simply **286**) refers to the microprocessor and to all computers based on the Intel 80286 chip. This term includes such computers as the IBM AT, AT clones, AT compatibles and the IBM Personal System/2 Models 50 and 60 and PS/2 clones.

**80386** (or **386**) refers to the microprocessor and all computers based on the Intel 80386 chip. This term includes such computers as the IBM Personal System/2 Model 70 and 80, along with all other 386-based computers including the newest PS/2 clones and compatibles.

# Evaluating the 8088-Based Computer

Many people are undecided about whether to go with an 8088
(XT type) or a 286 (AT type) computer. There are still very
good reasons for some users to purchase an 8088 rather than a
more expensive AT or 386 computer. Although the technology
for the XT is no longer the cutting edge, it may very well do
what you need it to do quite adequately, and also quite cheaply.
Buying a computer is little different from buying a new car. You
want to get the best performance for the best price. You
wouldn't buy a racing car if all you wanted to do was drive
around town. Similarly, you wouldn't buy a superfast computer
with all the trimmings if all you wanted to do was word processing or small business accounting.

In short, it makes no sense to buy an expensive overpowered
machine if neither your applications nor your wallet really need
it. The following look at the pros and cons of the 8088 will help
you to decide if you are one of those people who only need an
XT computer.

## Advantages of the 8088

Go with the 8088 if you want to save money. Approximately a
two-to-one price ratio exists between the price of an AT clone
and XT clone. In many areas of the country, a "bare bones" XT
clone with monitor, one drive, and 256 K of memory can be
purchased for under $400 dollars. This low price seems to create
a strong motivation for the home computer user (and especially
for the first time buyer with a tight budget) to purchase this kind
of computer.

An XT clone is definitely adequate for many uses. Some types of applications which can now be adequately handled by it include word processing, small databases, small spreadsheet, and telecommunications programs. The person who doesn't require lightning speed or large amounts of memory for their applications software can find the XT clone a quite adequate computer.

## Disadvantages of the 8088

Newer software programs are pushing against the limits of memory and speed that the 8088 has to offer. Therefore, there is not much room to grow. The 8088 will not, for example, be able to use the OS/2 software and all its extra features. It also has difficulty (slows down) when handling the large and complex graphic software that is starting to become available. Its main disadvantage, however, is speed. The 8088 is slow when compared to succeeding generations of computers.

Even though the 8088-based computer has reached its limits, those who purchase one of these computers will not necessarily have to lament their decision when they need a more powerful computer and software. The XT clone can be upgraded to an AT clone by adding a new Baby AT motherboard. It could even be upgraded to a 386 computer, for that matter. The conversion to a 286 now costs about $450. However, prices are always dropping. In a year or two the cost may be under $200. The upgrade option will help breathe new life into any XT clone. The *IBM AT CLONE BUYERS GUIDE AND HANDBOOK*, (available by sending in the coupon in the back of the book) has instructions for doing the upgrade.

# Evaluating the 80286-Based Computer

Computers that are using the 286 microprocessor are becoming increasingly popular and sales of these computers are growing at a rapid rate. There are many good reasons why these computers are gradually becoming the predominant type of computer on the market.

## Advantages of the 286

It is important to remember that the 286 computer will continue to grow in capabilities. With the OS/2 operating system, it will be able to use large amounts of memory, which will allow for the use of more powerful and easier-to-use software. The average 286 computer operates at least two to three times faster than a 8088-based computer. Also, some of the newest 286-based machines compete in sheer processing power and speed with presently available 386 computers. This means that tasks can be done significantly faster. Prices are also dropping rapidly, thereby making them an ever more attractive option for the computer user.

There are many software programs and tasks which require at least a 286 computer to operate effectively. These include: OS/2, fast complicated graphics (such as Desktop Publishing, Computer Aided Design and Computer Aided Engineering), large databases, complex spreadsheets, multitasking, and multi-user situations. The 286 is therefore suitable for a wide variety of applications and with it you will be prepared for most future computing needs you may have.

## Disadvantages of the 286

While the 286 computers have many advantages, these computers are no longer the cutting edge. This generation of computer will in time slowly be eclipsed by its successor the 386 computer, which offers the promise of much greater features and capabilities.

Again, there is no need to worry about being left behind technologically with a 286 computer because it is possible to upgrade it to the next generation of computer very easily. At present, most 386-based computers are merely AT clones with 386 motherboards installed. All parts in the AT are usable with the typical 386 computer, so to upgrade can mean only replacing one part – the motherboard. Instructions for doing the upgrade are in the *386 COMPUTER BUYER'S GUIDE AND HANDBOOK* (available by sending in the coupon in the back of the book).

*Figure 2.2*    I told you that you could have saved money buying an XT clone

# Evaluating the 80386-Based Computer

With the great potential of the latest 386-based computers, should you consider the  purchase of one of these instead of an XT clone?  Let's take a look at some of the factors which should influence your decision.

### The Advantages of the 386

Presently, speed stands out as the 386's greatest advantage.  The 386-based computers now available are certainly fast, but not dramatically so.  The machines now available operate only 40 to 100% faster than the previous generation of computer.

### The Disadvantages of the 386

The possible drawbacks of the 386 start with the high price.  The price difference between the 386 and 286 system is about two to one and for an 8088 computer, about 4 to 1, so there is still a hefty premium to pay.

A hardware standard for 386-based computer has not yet been clearly established.  It looks as though IBM's PS/2 Models 70 and 80 with the Micro Channel will eventually prevail as a hardware standard due to its inherent ability to perform parallel processing (which speeds up the computer enormously).  Many other companies have released 386-based computers, but not all have followed the same design for adding expansion cards.  So far, I have seen several expansion slot designs.  If a standards war develops, then it would definitely make the purchase of a

386 less attractive. When buying a 386, you may end up with a computer that you paid a lot of money for, but cannot accept commonly available expansion cards.

While most 386 computers can use the same expansion cards as the 8088 and 286 computers, few dedicated 386 cards exist. There are actually only a few 386 memory expansion cards now available and they do not fit in all machines. Expansion cards will not start to proliferate until a hardware standard becomes established.

Several software manufacturers offer operating systems to take advantage of some of the 386's capabilities. However, until a widely accepted operating system is available which takes full advantage of this computer's capabilities, the massive possibilities of the 386 will not be utilized. It may be several years before a dedicated operating system is available.

Until a standardized 386 operating system is available, little application software can be written for this computer. The capabilities are again underutilized. The 386 will, however, run all of the present software now existing for the MS-DOS operating system.

## 386 Summary

If speed is paramount and translates into money saved, a 386 may be for you. The best advice for most users is to wait a year or more after any new product becomes available in order to let the bugs get worked out and a clear standard to be set. (For example, the first version of the 386 microprocessor had a bug in the arithmetic function and Intel had to replace thousands of faulty chips). It was also found that the commonly used Intel motherboard could not accept the 80387 math coprocessor. For the "pioneers" who purchased these computers, this was certainly an inconvenience. If you decide to go with a 386, I recommend reading the *386 COMPUTER BUYER'S GUIDE AND HANDBOOK*.

*Figure 2.3*    The first 386 pioneers really took some risks

# Price Comparison

An important factor in deciding which generation of computers to purchase is the element of affordability. The following is a comparison of the relative price ranges between the three generations of computers at the time of the latest revision of this book.

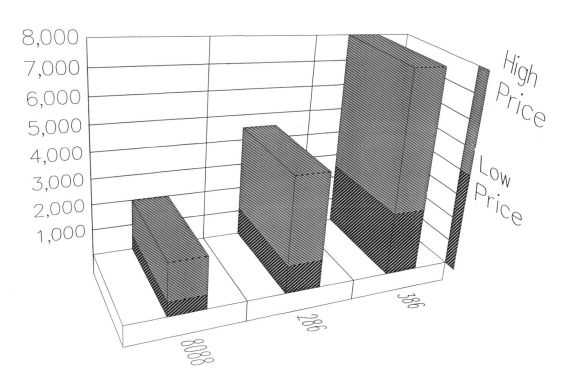

**Price Comparison of the 8088, 286, and 386 computers (in $)**

*Figure 2.4*   Comparing the price of computers based on each generation of chip

# Comparing the Technical Capabilities of the 8088, 286, and 386

For those of you who would like to understand the technical differences of the 8088, 286, and 386-based computers in a little more detail, the following text compares these computers in terms of speed, memory, multitasking, multiuser, and modes capabilities.

## Speed Capabilities

A faster computer can reduce the time you wait (while some task is being performed) from a few minutes to a fraction of a minute. Essentially, there are four factors which determine a computer's overall speed. These factors are as follows:

- "clock rate"

- "width" of data path

- overall efficiency of the microprocessor's design

- number of "wait states"

Before displaying a graphic comparison of the speed at which different generations of computers can operate, each of these factors will be briefly examined.

## Clock Rate

Inside the computer, a clock "ticks" at a constant rate. It is analogous to a metronome pacing the tempo of a piece of music. In the computer's case, the clock serves to pace the flow of data and thereby assists in keeping order among all the circuitry. The faster the clock, the faster data can be processed. The clock rate is measured in megahertz (MHz) or "million cycles per second." The higher the number of megahertz, the faster the speed. Each higher generation of computer can support a faster clock rate due to improved technology. There are also variations in the clock rate within each generation of CPU.

## Data Path

The data path in a computer can be likened to a freeway; the more lanes, the more traffic that can be carried. The wider the data path, the more information that can be manipulated.

- 8088 computers have an 8-bit data path ( 8 lanes)
  8086 computers have a 16-bit data path (16 lanes)

- 80286 computers have a 16-bit data path (16 lanes)

- 80386 computers have a 32-bit data path (32 lanes)

The majority of software now available has been written for 16-bit. Since the 8088 computers have only an 8-bit data path, the flow of data is reduced by about half. When 32-bit software becomes available for 386 computers, the processing speed will automatically be increased from two to four times, depending on the type of software. This extra speed is made possible by the wider data path.

*Figure 2.5*    **A narrow data path slows down traffic**

## Efficiency of Design

A degree of speed is gained in each new generation of computers due to improved efficiency of circuitry and overall design. Because the layout of the circuitry on the CPU is more efficient, the computer can process more data in less time. For this reason, the 286 chip is 2.5 times faster than the 8088 merely due to a better design. This means that an 8 MHz 286 is automatically 2.5 times faster than a 8 MHz 8088 chip. However, no difference in efficiency of design exists between the speed of a 16 MHz 286 chip and a 16 MHz 386 chip, provided they are using the same 16-bit software.

*Figure 2.6*　　Extra speed is gained in each generation of computer due to a better design

## Wait States

Wait states are placed between the CPU and RAM in an effort to slow down the transmission of data. They function similarly to pacing lights installed before a bridge or freeway – the lights turn on and off in an effort to regulate the flow of traffic. This process helps reduce traffic congestion just as the wait state reduces congestion in the computer's memory. Wait states were devised to allow slower (and thereby less expensive) memory chips to be used. When there is no wait state, the advantage is that data flows directly to and from the memory without waiting. The lack of wait states and the use of faster memory chips can increase the computer's speed by about 30%. (8088-based computers do not generally use wait states).

*Figure 2.7*     The lack of wait states can speed up the computers operation

There are actually several scales for measuring the speed of computers. The most accurate measures how many Millions of Instructions can be processed Per Second. This is referred to as MIPS. This measurement is used on all computers from mainframes down to microcomputers. However, the more common speed ratings you will see in advertisements are the ***Norton SI*** and the ***Landmark Speed Test***. The Landmark test is often used because it displays a nice graphic representation of speed in Megahertz relative to the AT. (The ***Landmark Speed Test*** is a public domain program and is available by sending in the appropriate coupon in the back of this book). The following graphs show a printout from the ***Landmark Speed Test***; first is an XT clone operating at 8 MHz, and the second is an AT clone operating at 10 MHz, 0 wait state.

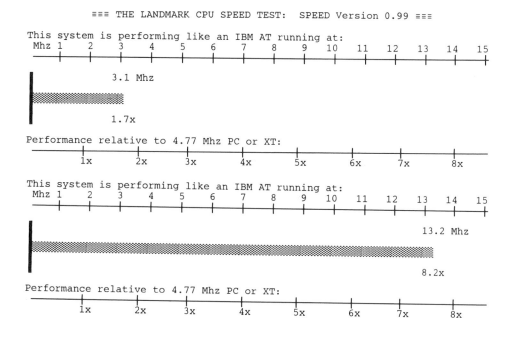

*Figure 2.8*   The ***Landmark Speed Test*** on an 8 MHz XT clone and on a 10 MHz, 0 wait state, AT clone

    The following chart compares the speed of the 8088, 286, and 386-based computers in megahertz relative to the AT using the same 16-bit software. (Remember, if 32-bit software were used, the 386 would be 2 to 4 times faster). Three different levels are shown. The first shows the speed of early computers using each chip operated. The second level shows the average speed at which computers currently operate, and the highest level shows the maximum speed capability of computers using each chip.

### Speed Of The 8088, 286, And 386 Computers (In MHz)

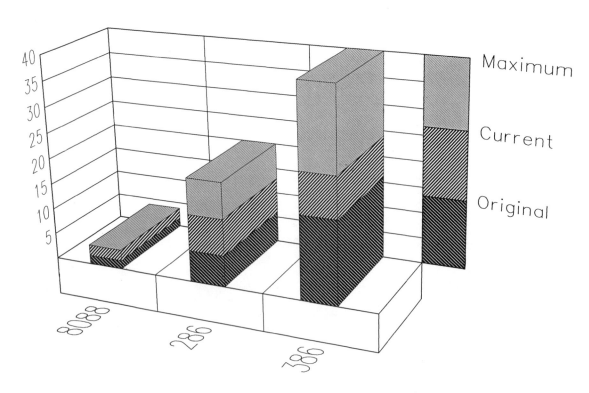

*Figure 2.9*    Comparing the speed of the 3 generations of computers

## Memory Capabilities

The term "memory" describes different forms of storing information. The two forms compared here are random access memory (RAM) and virtual memory. Before I go on though, it may be useful to explain how computer memory is measured.

| Definition of memory | | | |
|---|---|---|---|
| 1 bit | = | the smallest unit of information understood by the computer; it is represented as either "1" or "0", (also "on" or "off"). | |
| 1 byte | = | 8 bits | = | a character, i.e., A, 5, !, etc. |
| 1 Kilobyte | = | 1024 bytes | = | 1/2 page of text |
| 1 Megabyte | = | 1,000 Kilobytes | = | 500 pages of text |
| 1 Gigabyte | = | 1,000 Megabytes | = | 2 full sets of encyclopedias |
| 1 Terabyte | = | 1,000 Gigabytes | = | 2,000 full sets of encyclopedias! |

## Random-Access Memory (RAM)

RAM comprises the computer's main memory and is used for the temporary storage of data in memory chips. The following chart compares the inherent capabilities of CP/M, 8088, 286, and 386 computers in terms of their ability to access RAM. (CP/M is included here to help dramatize the rapid increase in the ability of each generation of computer to access RAM).

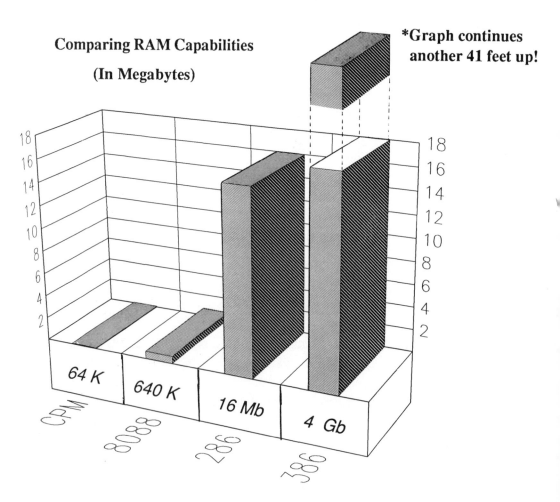

*Figure 2.10*    The amount of RAM each generation of computer can access

With more RAM available, larger and increasingly complex software can be used. An example of how the quantity of RAM can affect your actual computing would be to consider CP/M-based computers which can access only 64 K of RAM. This just barely allows the use of a word processing program. However, 64 K of RAM is not sufficient to allow the use of a spelling checker or a thesaurus. The 640 K memory in 8088-based computers opened the door for these time-saving programs. It also allowed the development of desktop publishing software. When the new OS/2 operating system makes available the full 16 Megabytes of RAM for the 286, it will be possible to merge desktop publishing programs with powerful word processing programs. Actual word definitions, which can be rapidly accessed, will also be incorporated into memory-resident diction-ary and thesaurus programs. What the 4 gigabytes of the 386-based computer will be used for is anybody's guess. Perhaps there will be some wild artificial intelligence programs which directly translate human thoughts into perfect, informa-tive, and interesting text. That could be of enormous use to poor laboring writers.

## Virtual Memory

As previously mentioned, a software program is dependent on the amount of RAM available. Greater amounts of RAM allow for larger and more sophisticated programs to be operated. Virtual memory (simplistically speaking) is a technique in which the computer accesses other memory, like those on a hard drive, and treats it as RAM. Large programs are therefore not limited to the availability of random access memory. This technique is relatively new for microcomputers, although it has been employed for years in large mainframe computers. The following chart compares the amount of virtual memory which each generation of computer will be capable of supporting when the proper operating systems are available.

**Virtual Memory of the 8088, 286,  and 386 computers**

**(In  Terabytes)**

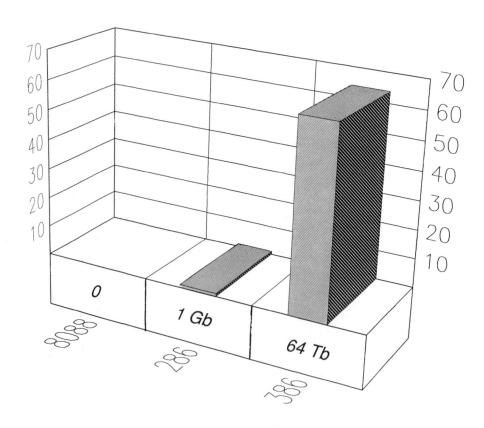

Figure 2.11    Comparing virtual memory capabilities

Initially, virtual memory will not be of significance to the average user. The first uses will be for large and complex multitasking and multiuser applications. It will, however, eventually open the door to new types of artificial intelligence programs that offer far better human interfaces than does present software. For a program to operate with minimum effort from the user's point of view, it needs to access large amounts of data rapidly. An example might be a voice recognition program which needs to understand many spoken words in a wide variety of circumstances.

*Figure 2.12*    Virtual memory will open the door to labor saving artificial intelligence programs

## Multiuser Capabilities

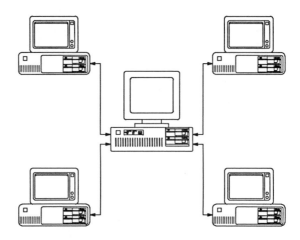

Multiuser simply means that you have two or more computers connected together which share information and/or peripherals. Generally, several computers are connected to one central computer (called a file server) which has a large and fast hard drive. The information contained in the file server is then shared among all the other computers or terminals. Special software and hardware are required to connect computers together. As of today, however, there is no industry standard for connecting computers, resulting in much confusion for potential users.

The 8088-based computer was not designed for multiple users and for all practical purposes cannot act as a file server. The 286 and 386-based computers, due to their superior design, are a prime choice for use as file servers. However, for the average user, connecting computers is not an important issue.

## Multitasking Capabilities

Multitasking means that multiple programs are operated at the same time by the computer. For example, while a database program is searching for a record, a complicated spreadsheet could be calculated, and the user could be writing a letter with the word processor, all at the same time. With multitasking, if several programs are simultaneously being operated, the computer does a piece of one...stops, does a piece of the next...stops, does a piece of the next job, and so forth. Because this process takes place very quickly, it looks to the user as if the various tasks happen at the same time. On the other hand, multiprocessing or concurrent processing (which is found on mainframe computers) means that two or more tasks are done **exactly** at the

*Figure 2.13*    A multiuser and multitasking environment

same time. There's no stopping and switching between tasks. This takes specially designed or parallel processors which work at the same time.

Multitasking in its present form is not very popular. This is due to the fact that the rather limited and awkward operating system (Microsoft's MS-DOS) is designed to be a single task/stand alone operating system. It does not lend itself well to multitasking. With OS/2, however, the 286 machines have a real advantage over the 8088-based machines because they operate faster and their chips are designed to do multitasking more efficiently. The 386 computers will really shine in this application because the 386 chip is specially designed to do multitasking.

*Figure 2.14*    Human multiprocessing with parallel processors

# Modes

Each generation of computer has the capability of supporting different "modes" of operation. These modes are referred to as "real mode," "protected mode," and "virtual 8086 mode."

## Real Mode

The 8088/86-based computer can operate in just one mode; this is referred to as real mode. In real mode, the computer can access 640 K of physical memory. MS-DOS exploits real mode, and the overwhelming majority of application software is written for this mode.

## Protected Mode

The 286-based computer can operate in real mode as well as in an added mode of operation called 286 protected mode. This protected mode allows for the access of 16 Megabytes of physical memory and 1 gigabyte of virtual memory. It also allows the ability to do multitasking more efficiently. When doing multitasking, the individual tasks are protected from each other so that if one locks up, it does not effect the other programs, hence the name "protected" mode. (When doing multitasking in real mode, if one program locks up, the entire computer would lock up, causing you to lose all your work). Presently, the problem with protected mode is that all existing software must be rewritten to take advantage of it. Microsoft's OS/2 has been designed to take advantage of the protected mode, however, few applications programs are available yet.

## Virtual 8086 Mode

The 386 computer can operate in real mode and in an
enhanced 386 protected mode which allows the access of 4
gigabytes of physical memory and 64 terabytes of virtual
memory. The 386 also supports one added mode called virtual
8086 mode. Under this mode, you can create many independently operating *"virtual 8086 machines"* on your one
computer. In other words you can set up separate virtual (or
imaginary) computers each working within a different window
on the same computer. You can then load an array of programs
written for the 8088 computer into each virtual machine and
switch from one program to the other. The advantage of virtual
8086 mode is that all previous software can be operated and you
can also do efficient multitasking. **Windows 386** by **Microsoft** is
a program which takes advantage of virtual mode and allows the
creation of multiple virtual machines.

**CHAPTER 3**

# WHICH XT COMPUTER IS BEST?

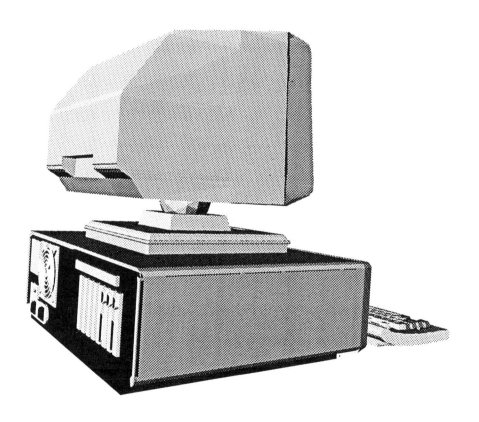

# Chapter Focus

This chapter divides the computers which
are based on the 8088 microprocessor into
four general categories. Each category is
then evaluated according to the issues of
compatibility, performance, price, reliability,
availability of support, potential for inter-
changing parts, expansion capabilities,
upgrade-path ability, potential for custom
designing the computer, and availability of
computer repair.

*Figure 3.1*    Preparing to judge the different computers

\* \* \* \* \*

AT THIS POINT, you may have decided that an 8088-based
computer is the appropriate machine for your needs.  There are,
however, so many of these particular computers available that
the buyer often feels a bit confused and overwhelmed by all the
choices. What's the difference?  Are they all alike?  The purpose
of this chapter is to begin sorting out the different 8088-based
computers which are available.

First, almost all 8088-based computers are similar in that they
have IBM software compatibility.  One major area where they
differ is in their physical design.  The best way to start, therefore,
is to arrange the computers according to their physical charac-
teristics.  Using this as the criteria, these computers can be
divided into four general groups or categories.  These categories
are as follows:

❏ **IBM XT**   This is the original 8088-based computer which became the industry standard for its generation.

❏ **XT Clones**   These computers are hardware interchangeable with the original IBM XT. In fact, every part of the IBM XT clone can be installed into a IBM XT and vice versa.

❏ **XT Compatibles (includes IBM Personal System/2 Models 25 and 30)**   This group deserves to be divided into two further subcategories:

☛ The first group consists of computers which use custom designed motherboards, power supplies, chassis, etc. and are, therefore, not totally hardware interchangeable with the IBM XT.

☛ The second group is referred to as passive backplane or sometimes as "motherboard-less" computers. These compatibles use a modular concept and place the chips (which are typically on the motherboard) onto an expansion card that plugs into a series of expansion slots.

❏ **Laptops (or portables)**   These computers have a small custom design, allowing them to be portable. This group is a vast topic in itself and as a result, is not covered in this book.

## Evaluating the Categories

In making your decision about which category is best for your needs, it is helpful to consider the issues having to do with the purchase of a computer.

# Evaluating the

|  | Software Compatible | Hardware Compatible | Performance | Price | Reliability |
|---|---|---|---|---|---|
| **IBM XT** | Excellent | Excellent | Poor | Poor | Poor to Fair |
| **XT Clones** | Fair | Excellent | Excellent | Excellent | Poor to Fair |
| **Compatibles PS/2 25 & 30** | Fair | Poor | Fair to Excellent | Poor to Fair | Poor to Fair |

In the following chart and text, these issues are defined and reviewed according to each of the four computer categories. The ratings are excellent, fair, and poor.

# Computer Categories

| Support | Interchange-ability | Expansion | Upgrade Path | Customizing | Repair |
|---------|---------------------|-----------|--------------|-------------|--------|
| Fair | Excellent | Excellent | Excellent | Fair | Excellent |
| Poor to Excellent | Excellent | Excellent | Excellent | Excellent | Excellent |
| Poor to Excellent | Poor | Poor to Excellent | Poor | Poor to Fair | Poor to Fair |

# Compatibility

Compatibility refers to the ability of software and hardware to function together without problems.  There are several types of compatibility.  They are as follows:

## Software Compatibility

The original IBM XT is the benchmark against which compatibility is measured.  The IBM XT was (as has already been stated) designed using parts which are readily available from many sources.  Any electrical engineer can purchase these parts and design a computer like the IBM XT.  The one part IBM has a copyright on is a chip called the *"BIOS"* (Basic Input/Output System).  The code written in the BIOS is the essence of compatibility (see page 198 for an in-depth discussion of the BIOS).  In order for software to function properly, it has to find certain instructions in the BIOS.  If the instructions are different or absent, the software will not operate correctly.

Software compatibility is no longer the issue it once was. Even the worst companies' BIOS have relatively good software compatibility to IBM.  Software developers want the broadest use of their software, which means larger sales and higher profits for them, so they write it with compatibility to the broadest base of computers in mind.

## Hardware Compatibility

Hardware compatibility refers to the ability of add-on parts to work with the computer.  Some expansion cards, especially EGA and memory cards, conflict with the BIOS of some computers.

When this occurs, the best solution is to try a different BIOS or use a different card. Hardware manufacturers wish to sell their products to as many people as possible, and therefore try to design their products to function with the broadest range of computers available.

*Figure 3.2*    Many different kinds of incompatibilities can exist

## Compatibility Between Software

Some programs will not coexist with other software programs regardless of what computer they operate on. The most typical conflicts between programs are those that are "RAM resident," such as desktop organizer or utility programs. These conflicts have nothing to do with the computer, but are the fault of the software.

## Compatibility Between Add-on Cards

Sometimes incompatibilities can exist between individual expansion boards. This again, has nothing to do with the computer itself. It has to do with the fact that there are two expansion cards which conflict with each other. In this case, it may be necessary to replace one of the cards or change the settings.

## Speed-Related Compatibilities

Some programs are written to operate at a certain speed. If you try to operate them on a faster computer, they may not function properly. The program could possibly lock up or will operate more rapidly than is appropriate (this is especially true for many computer game programs). Copy protected software also may not run at higher speeds; one more reason for avoiding copy protected software. Problems of this sort are usually resolved by switching to a lower speed or by using a utility program which slows down the computer. (One such program is in the Utility Disk and is available by sending in the software coupon in the back of this book).

## How They Rate

The IBM XT and PS/2 Model 25 and 30 are the computers that have the best software compatibility since they are the standard by which compatibility is measured. While still software compatible to the old XT standard, the hardware of the IBM Personal System/2 Model 25 and 30 is of a different design. This is what causes these computers to receive the rating of "poor" under hardware compatibility.

The software compatibility of clones and compatibles is constantly improving. For the moment, these computers are in the same league when it comes to software compatibility with the IBM standard. They have been designed to get as close to the IBM design as is legally possible. Unlike the XT clones, as was previously stated in this book, compatibles are not totally hardware interchangeable with the IBM XT; therefore, they have received a "fair" rating in this category.

Incompatibilities can arise on any computer. Since the most important element of compatibility has to do with the BIOS, the closer it is to the original XT, the better. Fortunately, the codes in the BIOS are constantly being improved and refined. If a compatibility problem is found, the BIOS can easily be replaced in order to resolve that problem.

# Performance

Performance essentially means how much work can be done in a given amount of time. This is primarily determined by the speed of the computer, but is also affected by the software, hard disk speed, internal memory management and the presence or absence of a math-coprocesor.

### How They Rate

To survive, the clone and compatible manufacturers, have had to offer better performance than IBM. As a result, clone and compatible makers have typically been first with new technology. When the IBM XT was running at 4.77 MHz, the clones and the compatibles were running at 8 and even 10 MHz. If you are contemplating the purchase of a 8088-based computer, you are probably doing it because you want an inexpensive reliable machine. However, it also makes sense to get the fastest machine possible. Virtually all XTs sold now are switchable from 4.77 to at least 8 MHz or higher. For that reason, it does not make sense to purchase a single speed, slow 8088 computer. At this point in time, 8 or 10 MHz computers are the best price/performance 8088s available.

*Figure 3.3*    Not everyone cares about performance

# Price

For most buyers, the key issue is price. For the individual who is using his or her own money, this is a primary concern. For individuals who are using a company's or institution's money, it is often not as relevant a factor.

Computers depreciate quickly. For this reason, it is not advisable to buy the most expensive computer available. Computer technology is changing so fast that in a couple of years, your wants and processing needs will likely outgrow your present computer, no matter which one you buy. The high performance computer of today will be "old hat" tomorrow and the resale value will likely be very low. You don't want to invest sizable amounts of money for a machine which may become obsolete after a few years. It is better to shop for something inexpensive, taking advantage of the low price, while meeting your present application needs.

Companies and individuals are in the same situation when it comes to resale value. Many larger companies have, until recently, used the following lines of reasoning: "We have to buy the IBM computers because insurance companies will only insure IBMs and the problem with clones is that they have no resale value." Neither of these arguments, however, is valid. Insurance companies will insure just about anything, and resale values (as already pointed out) are not good, no matter which machine you go with. Companies which purchased IBM PCs are now finding that no one wants these computers since they are technologically out of date. Even when a buyer can be found, their value is very low due to lack of demand. The same reasoning can be applied to any computer on the market. For this reason, again it is better to get a lower-cost computer than the most expensive one.

## How They Rate

In order to survive, every other computer manufacturer must have a lower price and greater capabilities than the IBM counterpart. The compatible makers generally price their computers just under IBM's while the XT clones typically are even lower in price. XT clones are now available at extremely low prices. Since XT clones are the lowest-cost 8088 computers available, price makes a strong argument in their favor.

*Figure 3.4*    "Hey buddy, how much did you pay for your computer?"

# Reliability

Generally speaking, reliability has replaced compatibility as the primary issue. Reliability has to do with how trouble free your computer is. You don't want to purchase a computer that is prone to failure and needs to be taken back to the dealer or manufacturer for repairs. The variable that determines whether a computer is reliable or not is the quality of the individual parts.

## How They Rate

Even the IBM XT has had its share of problems and for that reason, rates the same as clones and compatibles. My standards may be a little harsh in this respect, but I have seen far too many problems with all types of computers.

IBM claims the PS/2 series has greater reliability than any previous computers. Unlike its predecessors, which were designed using already available computer chips, the PS/2 series is completely designed and controlled by IBM. All the chips are custom designed to work together. The design requires no cables (often a source of problems) and no DIP switches to be set (again a common problem area). The chips use the latest technology and have a lower power consumption resulting in less heat (heat can wear out components).

The reliability for compatibles and clones varies a great deal, from very poor to excellent, because there are so many different manufacturers and parts available. The wide variety of available parts means that, of course, there are some low-grade computer parts on the market. The parts section (Chapter 6) is especially designed to assist you in getting the best value and parts for your money.

# Availability of Support

Good support means that information and service are readily available. In other words, when you need help with the computer, there should be a ready source for the help. The type of support you may need would include how to set configuration switches, connect a printer, expand the computer, format the hard drive, etc. When buying a computer system, it must be remembered that hardware support is different from software support. If software is purchased separately from the hardware, it is the responsibility of the software vendor to support what he sells.

Typically, hardware support can be supplied by good documentation, the dealer, the manufacturer, books, magazines, and user groups. The first line of support is the documentation which comes with the computer. The better the manuals, the easier it will be to set up and operate the computer. It should also be kept in mind that the more books and magazines available which cover the specific computer's operations, the better for the user.

Direct support essentially depends on the dealer; very seldom do you deal with the manufacturer. For this reason, it is important to purchase from a reliable dealer. Also, if the computer model is common enough, then user groups which support it are likely to exist; user groups make an excellent support resource.

## How They Rate

Support varies widely among the different categories of computers. Some compatible makers, for example, give excellent support while other compatible makers give poor support. The

*Figure 3.5*    Unusually good dealer support

same is true for clone computers. Of particular interest, perhaps, is the fact that some of the compatibles (such as Kaypro or Tandy) have a large enough following to have magazines and user groups formed to support them.

IBM will sell support for their computers in the form of a service contract. This type of support is, however, geared towards the corporate client. For individuals (from what I have heard), the support is not so good. It is always awkward to deal with bureaucracy and the very bureaucratic IBM is often slow to provide assistance to individual users. Since IBM no longer sells or promotes the XT, support is not as readily available as it once was. These computers therefore receive a "fair" rating.

A major complaint about XT clones that you may have heard is that support is often minimal. Frequently, clone dealers sell their products as if they were commodity items like hats or vegetables and the dealers themselves may have only a limited technical knowledge of computers. This complaint, however, could be directed at any computer dealer. It is actually possible to get more support from a clone dealer than from one who sells IBM's and/or compatibles. There are certainly unethical dealers selling clones (just as there are for any type of item that is on the market). When choosing a dealer, you have to be careful.

You should also be aware that with some clone purchases, the manuals are sometimes sketchy and written in poor English (obviously translated from Chinese or Japanese text in a poor fashion). One major advantage of the clones, however, is that their various parts are all nearly identical to IBM's; the reference manuals and books written on particular IBM computers can, therefore, also be used for their clones. For assured support, buy a computer which is widely available; buy from a local and reputable dealer and insist on a warranty period of at least one year.

# Potential for Interchanging Parts

It is important to purchase a computer for which replacement parts are readily available. This availability affects the ability to successfully carry out such tasks as expansion, upgrading, and repairs of the computer.

### How They Rate

A big advantage of the XT clones is that all parts are interchangeable with the IBM XT. This means that parts are readily available and will continue to be available due to the huge installed base of these computers.

*Figure 3.6*    It is important to purchase a computer for which the proper replacement parts are readily available

There are not yet many parts readily available for the PS/2 series and it may be quite a while until they are available.

One factor to consider, if you are wish to purchase a compatible like those from Epson, Leading Edge, Kaypro and the rest, is that with computer competition being so tough, there is a good chance that a manufacturer may be forced to drop or change its line because of low profit margins or low sales volume. The market is being flooded with both compatibles and clones, causing stiff competition among dealers. Many compatible and clone dealers will not be able to survive. One advantage to buying an XT clone is that parts for clones are so common and inexpensive you will have no problem finding replacement parts, service and expansion accessories at a reasonable cost. This is true even if the specific manufacturer or dealer you bought your computer from goes out of business. On the other hand, if a compatible computer line were to go out of business, you might end up needing specially engineered replacement parts, which could be difficult and almost certainly very expensive to obtain. Also, it should be kept in mind that if a line is discontinued, the dealer from whom you purchased the computer will probably not want to tie up capital in these spare parts. Many people respond to this by saying, "Ah, but Epson, Leading Edge, Kaypro, etc. are very large companies; they are not going to drop their lines of computers."

Not true! Well-known companies dump models all the time. Epson has dropped the QX-10 and QX-16; Leading Edge has discontinued its Model M; IBM is no longer manufacturing the PC, PC Jr., XT, XT286, and AT ; Kaypro dropped its CP/M machines; Apple scuttled the Apple III—to name but a few. With time the long list that already exists, most surely, will continue to grow.

# Expansion Capabilities

The computer field is changing very rapidly. New features are being developed all the time. For this reason, your computer should have ample room for expansion so that it can incorporate new features as they become available. Nothing is more frustrating than wanting to expand the computer only to find that it has reached its upper expansion limits.

Expansion capabilities are essentially based on three factors. These are:

**The number of expansion slots**    These slots provide the means for adding cards. Eight expansion slots are usually adequate for the average user.

**The power supply capacity**    The larger it is, the greater the number of add-on features you can have. A range of between 135 to 180 watts is usually satisfactory, depending on the type of computer.

**The number of 1/2 height drive bays**    This is where floppy drives, hard drives, tape back-ups, and CDROM's (Compact Disks Read Only Memory), etc. are mounted. Five drive bays should be the minimum. Also, the more that are directly accessible from the front, the better. Sometimes part of the case covers the drive bays and makes them inaccessible from the front. This means that they cannot accept removable storage devices like floppy disks, streaming tape, or optical disks.

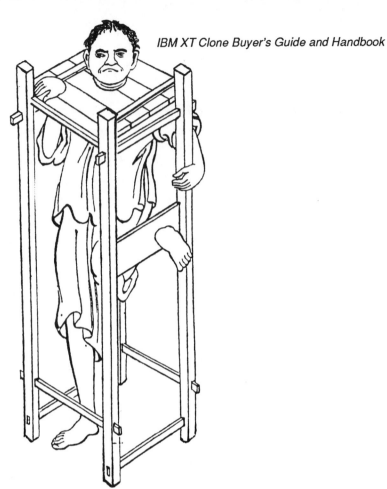

*Figure 3.7*    Leave yourself as much expansion room as possible

## How They Rate

The IBM XT, its clones and most compatibles, all have fairly good expansion capabilities. There are a few compatibles which have less than 8 expansion slots (such as the PS/2 Model 25 and 30). Often, computer sales people tell prospective customers, "Six expansion slots and two drive bays, one for a floppy drive and one for a hard disk, are enough; that is all you will ever need." But again, this ignores the many new applications being developed which require expansion cards (and slots) and/or extra drives.

# Upgrade Path Potential

The upgrade path refers to a computer's capacity to be upgraded from one generation of computer to the next generation; for example, an 8088 to a 286, or a 286 to a 386 computer, or even a 8088 to a 386. Having this option is one of the best solutions to avoiding computer obsolescence. It is, for example, possible to upgrade an XT computer to a Baby AT by changing the motherboard. This option is only readily available for computers which are true hardware clones of the IBM XT. The reason for this is that the installed base of the XT and its clones is so large that it is economically attractive for manufacturers to design 80286-based motherboards that will fit into an XT chassis.

## How They Rate

The upgrade option is not readily available for most compatibles because their hardware specifications are unique and their individual installed base is too small to make it worthwhile for third-party manufacturers to make specific upgrade boards.

# Potential of Custom Designing Your Computer

Many people want a computer that suits a specific application or need. They want the total flexibility to specify each individual part which makes up the computer. In other words, they want a total custom fit.

## How They Rate

Generally speaking, compatibles and the actual IBM computers do not have the design flexibility when it comes to custom configuring the computer. These computers come standard with a given set of parts and therefore give you less ability to pick and choose. An example is the **Compaq**, which must be purchased with its far-from-perfect keyboard. As a result, many users find themselves having to purchase a replacement keyboard and having to throw out the original.

On the other hand, the XT clone configuration is the most flexible one where in many instances the user can actually pick and choose hardware to custom match his or her needs. There are hundreds of companies which make their own versions of each part, so buying a clone can be likened to a smorgasbord. You can buy the keyboard you like or the monitor you like, etc. You can choose expensive, high-quality parts or buy lower-cost components and then exchange or expand the parts at a later time.

# Availability of Computer Repair

Computer repair is for some people a fearful topic. For a business or a professional, a computer failure can be a nightmare because important data and time can be lost. An entire business could actually come to a halt. It is, therefore, important to know how easily, quickly, and inexpensively the computer can be repaired.

## How They Rate

Because parts for IBM XT and clones are readily available and because most of them fit and work the same way from model to model, these computers are relatively easy and inexpensive to repair. Computer repair shops which can repair IBM computers can also repair clones; this is especially true because the parts are all interchangeable.

For do-it-yourself repairs, the IBM XT and the clones are probably the easiest computers to service. Anyone can swap a few parts to determine which one is defective. With the money saved by purchasing inexpensive clones (over IBM machines), a company could purchase a few extra machines for standby purposes. Because parts are so inexpensive and labor costs are so high, it is often less expensive for you (the individual user) to determine which part is bad and replace it yourself. New parts can be ordered by mail or bought from dealers. Computer magazines contain page after page of parts advertisements. Also, at computer swap meets, there are booths-upon-booths selling replacement parts of every description.

The passive backplane compatibles would be the easiest computers to repair, in terms of time. If the card containing the CPU

*Figure 3.8*    "I'm sorry your computer is broken.  What you should do is turn to Chapter
Eight to learn how to fix it "

were as readily available as the XT clone motherboard, it would
win hands down.  Unfortunately, the difficulty of finding low-
cost CPU cards makes this not yet the case.  This modular design
is what most electronic equipment tends toward because of its in-

herent efficiency. If any part fails, it can be quickly removed and a new one plugged in within minutes. It is a shame that IBM did not start out with this design and force it to become the industry standard.

Repairing a compatible could be significantly more expensive than a clone because it usually must be done by an authorized service representative who may need to use original replacement parts. These parts tend to be more expensive than standardized parts. Often, the marketing approach for compatible makers is to sell a computer at a low price now but make up for it later by charging an "arm and a leg" for repairing or upgrading it. The computer is also often sent (when being repaired) to an authorized service center and may be gone for two or more weeks, which could be a great inconvenience for some users.

Because of the newness of the PS/2 series, there are not yet many service technicians experienced with these computers. Also, replacement parts are not readily available so the computer must be repaired by an authorized service center. This repair, I suspect, will not be cheap.

## Summary

While each category of computer has its merits, it appears that the XT clones are about the best buys available when price, performance, upgradability, and interchangeability of parts are considered.

**CHAPTER 4**

# REVIEWS

# Chapter Focus

The following chapter consists of reviews of some of the most popular 8088 and 8086-based computers available. The reviews are divided into three categories: IBMs, compatibles, and clones.

The first part of each review discusses a few things about the company which manu-factures the computer. Next, comes a list of specifications, then the pros and cons of purchasing that particular machine.

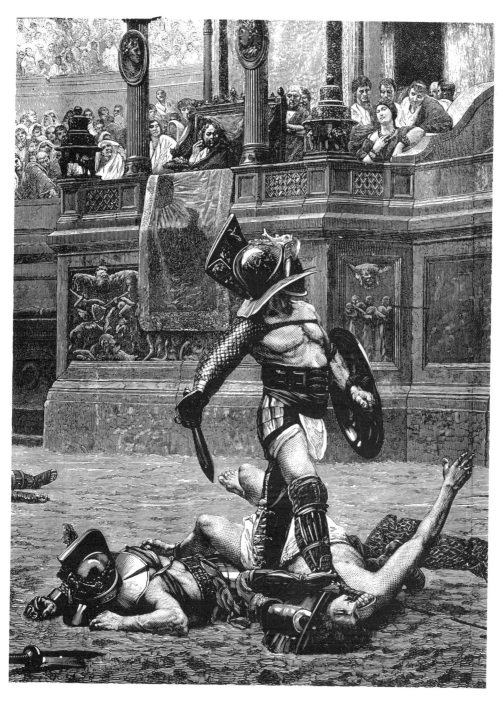

*Figure 4.1*    In the computer arena only the strongest  survive

\* \* \* \* \*

I N REVIEWING the 8088-based computers, I have chosen to
concentrate on some of the most popular machines now on the
market.  This review chapter is designed to simply give you an
idea of some of the particular choices available and how each of
these choices sizes up.

I would like to stress that these reviews are simply the
judgments which I and my research staff have come up with
during the process of writing this book.  These conclusions are
based on my own idea of what an "ideal 8088 computer" should
be.  I would like to emphasize that I am in no way claiming to be
some final authority on this topic; everyone has his or her own
opinions and aesthetic preferences.  You as the computer buyer
must ultimately be the judge of what is acceptable according to
your individual needs, wants, desires, and expectations.  These
reviews will at least give you a framework within which to judge
the various computers on the market.

The reviews covered in this chapter are general statements about the computers at the time this book went to print. Manufacturers do not necessarily, however, always use the same parts forever. Substitution of parts could affect the assessment of the particular computer as a whole. Before purchasing any computer, it is best to ask the computer vendor what parts are currently being used. Chapter 6, Understanding the Parts, can be used as a guide in this matter.

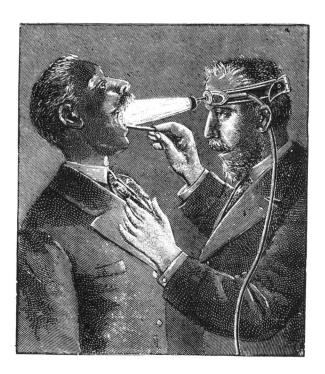

*Figure 4.2*    It's time for a close up examination

# IBM

IBM is one of the largest companies in the world, having sales in excess of $50 billion a year, and over 400,000 employees. It is the number one computer maker in the world and is unquestionably the dominant force in the field of computers. IBM's size has given them the ability to create standards around each of the computer generations it has brought out. This ability to standardize the industry has worked, so far, to benefit computer manufacturers as well as to consumers. It means that the manufacturers must conform to a particular level of quality and capability in each of their products. It also means that there is a central line of products that all manufacturers must improve upon to remain competitive. Due to intense competition among the compatible and clone makers, there is a tremendous downward pressure on the price. Without a standard, there would be little compatibility between computers and software, and the prices would be prohibitive.

*Figure 4.3*    IBM executives have decided to bury the XT

# IBM XT

*Figure 4.4*    The *IBM XT*

The XT was IBM's second microcomputer after the PC.  It set the industry standard for 8088-based computers.  At this point in time, the IBM XT is no more.  Both the XT and AT have been discontinued by IBM because they want to push customers toward their new PS/2 computer line.

```
┌─────────────────────────────────────┐
│                                      │
│         IBM XT in brief              │
│                                      │
│   Type:            IBM XT            │
│   CPU/Speed:       8088/4.77 MHz     │
│   Landmark Speed:  1.7 MHz           │
│   Power Supply:    135 Watts         │
│   Max. Memory:     640 K             │
│   Drive Bays       Hidden:    0      │
│                    Open:      4      │
│   Expansion Slots: 8                 │
│                                      │
└─────────────────────────────────────┘
```

## Pros

❏ This computer has good expansion capabilities. It has 8 expansion slots, 4 open drive bays, and a large power supply.

❏ The documentation is thorough.

❏ Compatibility in not an issue since this is the original against which all the others are measured.

## Cons

❏ The IBM XT's speed is slower than the competition. It operates at 4.77 MHz while the competition is at 8, 10 or even 12 MHz.

❏ The XT is no longer being manufactured. IBM wants to push their new line of PS/2 computers instead of the clonable (and less profitable) XTs and ATs. This means support will be increasingly difficult and expensive to get.

❏ The price was too high; you could have bought two or three XT clones for the price of one IBM XT.

# Personal System/2 Model 25

*Figure 4.5* The *Personal System/2 Model 25*

The IBM PS/2 model 25 is IBM's "low-end" model of the PS/2 line. The computer itself is considerably smaller than any of the previous generation of computers or any of the current PS/2 line of computers. It uses an 8086 CPU chip running at 8 MHz, comes with 512 K and can be upgraded to 640K. IBM hopes to compete with Macintosh in the educational market with this computer, but is unlikely to do so since the machine's price is high. There are several different types including the Standard and Collegiate models.

```
           IBM PS/2 Model 25 in brief

   Type:              Compatible
   CPU/Speed:         8086/8 MHz
   Landmark Speed:    4.4 MHz
   Power Supply:      90 Watts
   Max. Memory:       640 K
   Drive Bays         Hidden:   0
   (3 1/2 inch)       Open:     2
   Expansion Slots:   2
```

## Pros

❑ The machine is relatively fast. The 8086 chip at 8 MHz moves data at a respectable clip.

❑ Comes with DOS 3.3, Windows, and mouse.

❑ Video, serial, parallel and mouse ports are built in.

## Cons

❑ There is no hard disk and one cannot be added internally.

❑ There are poor expansion capabilities with only two expansion slots.

❑ The price is very high.

❑ Is not upgradable to a 286 or 386-based computer.

# Personal System/2 Model 30

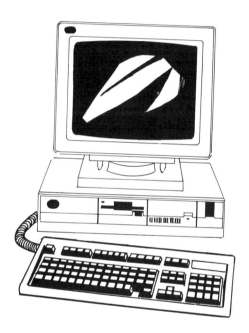

*Figure 4.6*    The *Personal System/2 Model 30*

The PS/2 Model 30 is much like the Model 25 except that it has a larger chassis and allows for more expansion.  Surprisingly, it is IBM's best seller even though it does not come with the much touted Micro Channel bus.

---

### IBM PS/2 Model 30 in brief

| | |
|---|---|
| **Type:** | **Compatible** |
| **CPU/Speed:** | **8086/8 MHz** |
| **Landmark Speed:** | **4.4 MHz** |
| **Power Supply:** | **70 Watts** |
| **Max. Memory:** | **640 K** |
| **Drive Bays** | **Hidden:  0** |
| **(3 1/2 inch)** | **Open:    2** |
| **Expansion Slots:** | **3** |

---

## Pros

❏ There are no dip switches or installation software, because the computer is self configuring.

❏ The power supply is small and its fan is quiet. Also, the power switch is conveniently located in front of the computer.

❏ There are many built-in features such a floppy controller, video display, serial port, parallel port, and a mouse port.

❏ The use of surface mount CMOS chips makes the machine more reliable.

## Cons

- ❏ The expansion capabilities are poor with only three empty expansion slots and only 2 drive bays.

- ❏ There is no upgrade path to a 286 or 386 computer.

- ❏ The hard disk that comes with this machine is remarkably slow.

- ❏ This computer is very expensive. You can buy at least two or three older model XT clones for the same price with similar performance. If you buy the Model 30, you're paying a premium price while getting less than premium performance.

*Figure 4.7*    I believe our search for the Divine would go faster with a 10 MHz Turbo XT clone with a V-20 chip.

# Epson

*Figure 4.8*     The *Epson Equity I Plus*

**Epson,** a division of the **Seiko Watch Company** of Japan, was the first company to produce and distribute a dot matrix printer. Their printers, in fact, have the largest share of the dot matrix printer market in the world. **Epson** became famous for this product and it still represents the bulk of their manufacturing product line. **Epson's** entry into the 8088-based computer market is called the ***Epson Equity I Plus.***

### Epson Equity 1 Plus in brief

| | |
|---|---|
| **Type:** | Compatible |
| **CPU/Speed:** | 8088/4.77-10 MHz |
| **Landmark Speed:** | 4.2 MHz |
| **Power Supply:** | 80 Watts |
| **Max. Memory:** | 640 K |
| **Drive Bays** | Hidden: 0 |
| | Open: 2 |
| **Expansion Slots:** | 5 |

## Pros

☐ It has a very stylish design with a certain charm.

☐ The computer is well built and is backed by a company with a good reputation for support and reliability.

☐ Dip switches are in front and easily accessible.

## Cons

☐ It has poor expansion with only two drive bays, 5 expansion slots and a small 80 watt power supply.

☐ There is no upgrade path to a 286 or 386 computer.

☐ No LED status lights on the front panel.

☐ The computer is relatively expensive when compared to other XT clones.

# Leading Edge

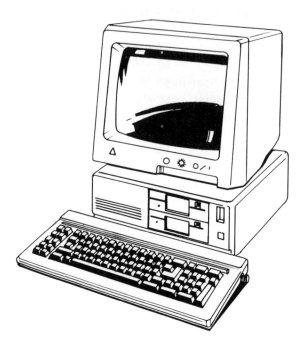

*Figure 4.9*    The *Leading Edge Model D*

Leading Edge of Massachusetts is a company which was initially
known for their word processing software.  They do not design
or assemble their own computer products but rather resell computers made by other manufacturers.  Their first offering, the
*Model M* was manufactured in Japan by *Mitsubishi* and sold
under the **Leading Edge** name.  **Leading Edge** and **Mitsubishi**
had heated disagreements which ended in lawsuits, so **Mitsubishi** stopped shipping this model.  **Leading Edge** in turn
found another supplier from South Korea.  This computer is from
the manufacturing giant, **Daewoo**, and is called the *Model D*.

```
┌──────────────────────────────────────┐
│       Leading Edge Model D in brief   │
│                                       │
│   Type:              Compatible       │
│   CPU/Speed:         8088/4.77 MHz    │
│   Landmark Speed:    1.7 MHz          │
│   Power Supply:      N/A Watts        │
│   Max. Memory:       640 K            │
│   Drive Bays         Hidden:   0      │
│                      Open:     2      │
│   Expansion Slots:   4                │
│                                       │
└──────────────────────────────────────┘
```

## Pros

❏  Stylish case with a small footprint.

## Cons

❏  Limited expansion capabilities, ie. only 2 drive bays and 4 expansion slots.

❏  Motherboard is not standard. A baby AT clone motherboard can not be placed in this machine, and so no upgrade path to an AT or 386 is possible.

❏  Service is reputed to be very poor.

❏  It operates at a very slow 4.77 MHz.

❏  This computer is presently losing popularity and may not be manufactured much longer. This possibility combined with its nonstandard features make the Model D a poor buy.

# Tandy

*Figure 4.10*    The *Tandy 1000 SX*

The **Tandy Corporation** of Fort Worth, Texas, was founded by David Tandy and David Hinckley in 1919.  **Tandy** owns and operates **Radio Shack Stores**, the nation's leading distributor of electronic equipment.  They were one of the first companies to make a personal computer, the *TRS-80* which came with its own operating system.  **Tandy** has now made the transition to MS-DOS systems and the IBM standard.

**Tandy Corporation's** contribution to the XT microcomputer market at present is the *Tandy Model 1000* series.  **Tandy** is bringing a new 8086-based computer out called the *1000 SL*.  It is much the same as the *1000 SX* except it is a bit more powerful.

```
┌─────────────────────────────────────────┐
│           Tandy 1000 SX in brief         │
│                                          │
│   Type:            Compatible            │
│   CPU/Speed:       8088/4.77-7.15 MHz    │
│   Landmark Speed:  2.9 MHz               │
│   Power Supply:    60 Watts              │
│   Max. Memory:     640 K                 │
│   Drive Bays       Hidden:  0            │
│                    Open:    2            │
│   Expansion Slots: 5                     │
│                                          │
└─────────────────────────────────────────┘
```

## Pros

❑ This computer has support from over 1100 **Radio Shack** computer stores.

❑ There is a built-in serial and parallel port.

## Cons

❑ There is no upgrade path to a 286 or 386-based computer.

❑ There is only a three month warranty. And here's the real killer: if you open up the computer within the warranty period, your warranty is voided. This could make expanding a **Tandy** system cost an arm and a leg, up to five times that of XT clone accessories.

❑ Poor aesthetics. Looks tacky.

❑ The keyboard is not interchangeable with the IBM standard, therefore you can't upgrade to a better keyboard later on.

❑ Initially, the basic systems price seems to be attractive. However, by the time you add the necessary elements for a useful working computer, the price is quite high.

*Figure 4.11*    Upgrading the Tandy computer could cost you and arm and a leg.

# Club American Technologies

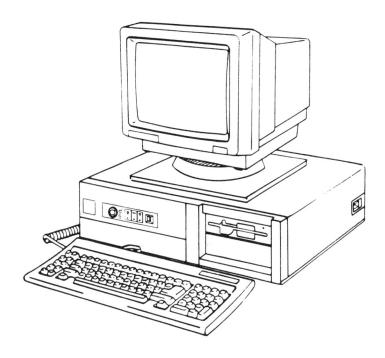

*Figure 4.12* The *Club American Technologies Model 110*

Located in Fremont, CA. **Club American Technologies** has been in business since 1984. The bulk of their activity is mail order and in 1988 they had $97 million is sales. They sell a wide variety of 8088, 286, and 386-based systems. The computer reviewed here is their entry level 8088-based computer called the *Model 110*.

**Club Model 110 in brief**

| Type: | XT Clone |
|---|---|
| CPU/Speed: | 8088/4.77-10 MHz |
| Landmark Speed: | 4.1 MHz |
| Power Supply: | 130 Watts |
| Max. Memory: | 640 K |
| Drive Bays | Hidden:  2 |
|  | Open:   2 |
| Expansion Slots: | 8 |

## Pros

❑ The price is competitive with other mail order firms and is backed by a solid company.

❑ System runs at 10 MHz and uses a DTK motherboard.

❑ It is upgradable to a 286 or 386 based-computer.

## Cons

❑ The computer has only two open drive bays and two hidden drive bays as does the IBM AT.

# Dell Computers

*Figure 4.13*    The *PC's Limited Turbo XT*

**Dell Computers**, previously known as **PC's Limited**, was founded in 1985 by Michael Dell, a pre-med student at the University of Texas in Austin. He became well-known for turning a garage operation into a large multi-million dollar mail order house. **Dell Computers** is now looking to change their image from a low cost mail order house to a more solid, corporate oriented organization. As part of this effort, they have changed their name to **Dell Computer Corporation**.

```
┌─────────────────────────────────────────┐
│                                          │
│      PC's Limited Turbo XT in brief      │
│                                          │
│    Type:            XT Clone             │
│    CPU/Speed:       8088/4.77-8 MHz      │
│    Landmark Speed:  3.1 MHz              │
│    Power Supply:    130 Watts            │
│    Max. Memory:     640 K                │
│    Drive Bays       Hidden:   0          │
│                     Open:     4          │
│    Expansion Slots: 8                    │
│                                          │
└─────────────────────────────────────────┘
```

## Pros

- ❏ Comes with a one year, on-site service contract from **Honeywell Bull** and a 30-day money-back guaranty.

- ❏ Can be upgraded to a 286 or 386.

- ❏ Has 4 open drive bays for easy access to removable storage devices.

## Cons

- ❏ There is no hardware switch for switching the speed.

- ❏ It is a rather plain looking computer.

- ❏ Their prices are higher since they are targeting the corporate market.

# Whole Earth Electronics

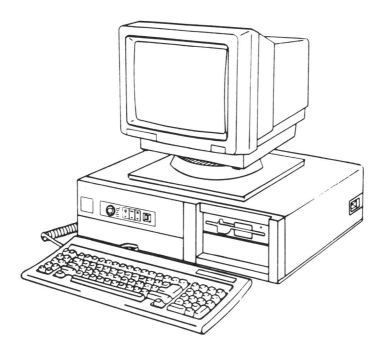

*Figure 4.14* The *Whole Earth XT*

**Whole Earth Electronics** is a relatively new entry into the clone market. They are a mail order division of the **Basic Living Products Company** of Berkeley, California. This is a multi-faceted company that also owns the four **Whole Earth Access Stores** in the San Francisco Bay Area. These stores gross in the vicinity of $50 million per year, selling anything from baby bottles to computers. **Whole Earth Electronics** sells a variety of computers.

```
┌────────────────────────────────────────┐
│          Whole Earth XT in brief        │
│                                         │
│   Type:            XT Clone             │
│   CPU/Speed:       8088/4.77-10 MHz     │
│   Landmark Speed:  4.1MHz               │
│   Power Supply:    150 Watts            │
│   Max. Memory:     640 K                │
│   Drive Bays       Hidden:    2         │
│                    Open:      2         │
│   Expansion Slots: 8                    │
│                                         │
└────────────────────────────────────────┘
```

## Pros

❑ This computer has a one year parts and labor warranty as well as a 30 day money back guaranty.

❑ The price is competitive with other mail order firms and is backed by a solid company.

❑ System runs at 10 MHz and uses the DTK motherboard.

❑ It is upgradable to a 286 or 386 based-computer.

## Cons

❑ The computer has only two open drive bays and three hidden drive bays as does the IBM AT.

# No-Name Clone Company

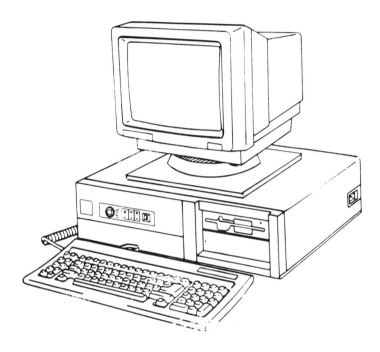

*Figure 4.15      A No-Name  XT Clone*

The thousands of companies who assemble and sell the "no-name" computer can be found in regular computer stores, small shops, garages, and basements all over the country.  The CEOs of these companies range anywhere from being the future computer tycoons of America to the future bankruptcy candidates.

The computers that these companies put out represent the largest portion of computers sold.  Their computers are made from parts which are manufactured all over the world.  Each company purchases their own blend of parts rolling them into a finished custom designed computer onto which they may place their own label or no label at all.  When buying this type of clone you need to be well-informed about what parts are being used in the computer.  You also need to purchase the computer from a reliable dealer.

### No-Name XT Clone in brief

| | |
|---|---|
| **Type:** | XT Clone |
| **CPU/Speed:** | 8088/4.77 - 12 MHz |
| **Landmark Speed:** | 1.7 - 4.5 MHz |
| **Power Supply:** | 130 - 180 Watts |
| **Max. Memory:** | 640 K - 1 Mb |
| **Drive Bays** | Hidden:  0 to 2 |
| | Open:     2 to 4 |
| **Expansion Slots:** | 8 |

### Pros

❏ This type of computer offers unbeatable low prices when compared to name brand compatibles and name brand clones.

❏ Some no-name clones use very good quality parts.

❏ They have good expansion features.

❏ They can be upgraded to a 286 or 386-based computer.

## Cons

- ❏ There is a wide range of parts quality; hence, there is the risk of purchasing poor quality parts.

- ❏ This type of computer requires more research and shopping time to obtain the best system for your needs. The better informed you are, the better your shopping results will be.

- ❏ The company or dealer may not be reliable, or even in business tomorrow thereby leaving you without a warranty.

*Figure 4.16*   The CEOs of these companies range anywhere from being the future computer tycoons of America to the future bankruptcy candidates

# CHAPTER 5

# WHERE TO PURCHASE THE COMPUTER

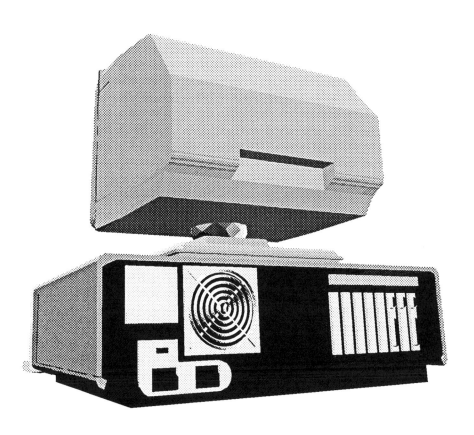

# Chapter Focus

The following chapter is a guide for the actual task of buying your computer or add-ons.  The chapter is divided into two parts.  The first part explains some general ideas and tips which should be kept in mind while buying.  The second part of the chapter takes a close look at the different source for buying.

*Figure 5.1*    A well-prepared computer shopper

\* \* \* \* \*

PERHAPS AT THIS point, you have decided to purchase an XT clone, but are unsure as to how to go about making this purchase. It is certainly a confusing situation with an overabundance of advertisements from retailers, dealers, consultants, mail order sources, etc. All claim they have the absolute best price and are the most reliable in the industry. Whom do you trust? The following are some tips on how to purchase an XT clone as well as any computer parts and accessories.

## First Be an Informed Shopper

While there is no ultimate answer to the question of where to get the "best deal," the best advice is "be an informed shopper."

Becoming informed consists of asking lots of questions and being willing to do a bit of research. To accomplish this, the first stop for many shoppers will be the public library. There, the prospective buyer can check out books on computers and read computer magazines. Going through the back issues of computer magazines and looking for articles on clones is a good way to get caught up on what's been happening in this field.

You can find fairly up-to-date computer books and magazines in book stores. It may be worth your while to purchase three or four leading computer magazines to check out the latest news and advertisements which will give you current national pricing. You can also take out a subscription to magazines you like the best. Many cities have locally-oriented tabloid computer magazines, which are available for free or at a very low price. Here you can compare advertisements of local computer dealers.

*Figure 5.2*    Study up on computers before buying

(A list of magazines relevant to clones can be found in Appendix C at the back of this book.)

Another good source of information is friends. Ask your friends who already own computers how they went about making their purchases. Where did they purchase their computers? How much did they cost? Were they satisfied with the machines and was the seller helpful to them? It might even be especially beneficial to have a friend go along with you when you go computer shopping; your friend can possibly assist you in asking the right questions.

It is also helpful to find computer users in the same profession as yourself and to ask about their experiences at buying. You might equally benefit by asking them how they make use of their computers in their work. Most professions have trade journals, which often have information on how computers are used in that field, for example, a lawyer's journal may discuss the merits of time billing software or a medical journal may discuss the use of computerized pharmaceutical data bases.

In many cities, computer users have joined together into groups to share information on computers. These user groups usually meet on a monthly basis and have a wealth of information on all aspects of computing. They may also be able to recommend vendors who have a good reputation. Most larger groups offer a newsletter with useful information. User group listings can be found in the back of local computer magazines. The nationally distributed **Computer Shopper** magazine has a listing of computer user groups, divided according to regions.

## Buy Locally if Possible

If possible, purchase your computer from a vendor near where you live, to allow for easy access to service and support. Buying locally is especially advantageous because you then cut down travel time and/or shipping costs, should your computer develop a problem.

*Figure 5.3* A typical user group meeting

## Check References

Of course, if you have friends who recently bought XT clones in a satisfactory manner, then those friends can refer you to the vendors they used. If you don't know anybody who has recently made such a purchase, you can then ask the vendor for the names of some of his recent customers. Checking references is one of the best ways to find out the dealer's reputation, and it will safeguard you from buying from the wrong person.

## How to Bargain

As with everything highly competitive, a free enterprise system drives the price to its lowest possible level. Computers are no exception. It is therefore, a buyer's market, which gives you some room for bargaining. To bargain, get a price quote from the first dealer, take it to a second dealer and ask if the price can be beaten. When bargaining, it is very important to watch out for the quality of parts which you are being offered. Make sure the prices that you're quoted are for the same parts or for the same quality of parts.

## Insist on a Good Warranty

A good warranty is the best initial insurance in the event of computer failure. Know the exact terms of the warranty and read all fine print before purchasing any computer. If hardware problems do occur, a "parts-and-labor" warranty covers both the cost of any replacement parts and labor charges. A "limited" warranty usually means that only parts will be replaced without cost, and you will be charged for any labor involved. Sometimes it's the other way around – free labor, but charged for parts that are to be replaced. A one-year full-parts-and-labor warranty is of course, the most preferable and is entirely reasonable.

The following are some specific questions which you should ask about the warranty:

☐ "What kind of warranty comes with the computer: full-parts-and-labor, or limited?"

☐ "What are the labor charges, if any?"

☐ "Are all parts under the same warranty?" Sometimes, certain parts have only a couple of months warranty, while others have as much as a full two years.

☐ "Will the dealer replace parts immediately, or will they be sent to the manufacturer for repair?" If they're sent to the manufacturer, you could be without a computer for several weeks. It is therefore, better if the dealer can do a direct parts swap on the premises.

# Don't Be Pressured

A few dealers use hard-sell techniques; don't let this pressure affect you. If you feel the dealer is using high pressure sales tactics, simply go to another dealer; there are generally plenty of clone dealers available. The most reasonable and intelligent thing to do is to check with several dealers before buying.

*Figure 5.4*    Don't be pressured by hard sell tactics

## Check Compatibility

As previously mentioned, software compatibility is no longer the problem it once was. Still, if you have some uncommon or specialized software which you intend to use, it doesn't hurt to try it out on the computer before making your purchase. If the dealer doesn't want to cooperate, it might be best to avoid buying from him.

## Check for FCC Approval

Federal Communications Commission (FCC) approval states that the computer has met its standards for radio frequency interference (RFI). This is especially important because the radio frequency emissions can affect other electronic devices which are being used nearby. The FCC has lately been cracking down on unapproved computers by issuing citations. This has meant that many clone makers and/or dealers who have previously seen the FCC approval as not necessary, are now scrambling to obtain FCC approval for their systems. A potential problem for owners of unapproved systems is that, legally, a dealer who sells computers without FCC approval could be forced to recall them. This could be an inconvenience for the buyer, to say the least. It seems advisable, when shopping, to keep this possibility in mind and look for the FCC approval sticker.

The process of gaining FCC approval makes it difficult for small dealers to comply. The FCC requires that the computer be tested by a private testing company. The testing fee can be as high as two thousand dollars. Once the computer passes, the test results must be sent to the FCC offices in Washington for final certification and this process takes several months. If during the approval process, the dealer installs new and improved parts into the computer, it must again be submitted for testing and the approval process starts from the beginning. The process is not set up for rapid changes in technology. In other words, the dealer is caught between a fast-moving market and a slow-moving FCC. For that reason, many small dealers have tended to completely forgo FCC approval.

It should also be kept in mind, that the FCC has two classes of certification. "Class A" designates approval for business use. "Class B" is more stringent and is for household use where radios and televisions that are to be operated near the machine could be affected.

You may also want to check for Underwriters Laboratories approval (UL approval). This is a private organization which determines the safety of high voltage electrical devices such as power supplies and monitors. UL approval does not replace the FCC approval; even with UL approval it is still necessary to also have FCC approval.

## Check for "Burn-In" Period

The term "burned-in" means that the computer has been tested by letting it run for several hours; some dealers routinely burn-in their unit up to 48 hours. The burning-in process helps catch many hardware problems which may otherwise have occurred during the initial use of the machine. Before purchasing the computer, ask the vendor how long it has been burned-in. The minimum time should be 12 hours.

# The Sources for Buying a Computer

Most computer vendors it seems are responsible and honest. In the San Francisco Bay Area, I so far have found only a handful of dealers (out of the hundreds here) to be unreliable. One of these dealers used unethical bait-and-switch tactics. The others sold poor quality equipment and didn't back it up. The first went out of business quickly. The latter ones, while still in business at the time this book went to print, are probably not far behind in their demise.

Several sources are available for the actual purchase of the computer. They can be divided them into 5 groups. These are: retailers, clone dealers, "garage dealers," computer shows, and mail order.

*Figure 5.5*   Be cautious when approaching dealers

## Computer Retail Stores

Computer retail stores are typically the larger store front computer outlets which have display windows and a more upscale look.  They are often chains such as **Computerland, Radio Shack, Businessland, Entre**, and **Nynex**.  The giant chains (such as **Computerland** and **Radio Shack**) don't usually carry clones, but rather carry brand name compatibles, which have a higher profit margin.

Retail stores charge the highest prices for computers.  This is because of their high overhead: rents, salaries, inventory expenses, etc.  Some buyers, especially larger companies, feel more secure buying from a retail store than from other sources.  This is because they feel comfortable with the fact that retail stores offer a local source for support, parts, service, advice and training in how to use the computer.  It should also be noted that they are often more knowledgeable about software than other sources.  On the other hand, there are many retail stores where the staff has minimal or no knowledge about their products.  Sometimes you may find you know more than the salesperson.  Unless you can find a retailer who offers exceptional service and support, it's usually preferable to buy from one of the other, lower-priced outlets mentioned in this chapter.

For location of computer retail stores that are near you, look in the yellow pages under computers, or look for their adds in the newspaper.

# Clone Dealers

What I refer to as "clone dealers" are computer dealers who tend to sell, almost exclusively, nothing but clones and clone accessories. In addition to these items, they sometimes will sell software. Their places of business are typically small, out-of-the-way places...an obscure shop, an office, or even a home. Often, these places are a bit dishevelled and are stacked to the ceiling with boxes of computers and parts. These dealers work with low overhead, and many of them import at least some of their parts directly from Asia. Due to low overhead, a clone dealer's price for an XT clone will usually be lower than a computer retailer's price for the same machine.

In general, clone dealers are quite responsible when it comes to supporting the hardware they sell; they don't want to get a bad reputation which would hurt their sales. If something should go wrong with the computer within the warranty period, the clone dealer will usually replace it without a quibble. This is especially true if they import the parts themselves. It should be kept in mind, however, that there are some clone dealers who offer little support beyond honoring their warranty while other clone dealers will offer a great deal of support, even more than you could possibly get in a retail store.

The best place for finding these clone dealers is at computer swap meets and shows. These meets and shows are held every few months in most major cities. Check in local computer tabloid magazines for the location and date of shows in your area.

Sometimes clone dealers advertise in local newspapers with small display adds, or in the classified ads under Computers For Sale. A typical clone dealer ad might read like these:

IBM XT clone. 640 K, 1DD, $495. Unused warnty, (555-1212)

IBM XT clone, new w/warr. $799. 1 Meg ser. par. 20 mg HD, all upgrades avail. ABC (phone no.)

## Garage Dealers

What I refer to as "Garage Dealers" are the many individuals who have found that they can assemble and sell XT clones from their homes, either as a full time job or as a sideline. Some of these dealers are by profession computer consultants and can offer excellent advice about the clones they sell. Some are students who sell to their fellow students and to their teachers. Some are employees of large companies who find a ready market among their many co-workers.

Garage dealers often get into the field by first building an XT clone for themselves, then for friends who want low-priced computers, but who do not want to do the assembly themselves. It doesn't take long and word-of-mouth often is all a garage dealer needs to get established. Once the garage dealer is selling a couple of computers per week, he or she can go to the clone dealers for parts at "dealer prices" and so work on the same cost level as computer retailers who sell clones. The number of garage dealers is mushrooming. Since there's no such thing as an "authorized" clone dealer, as there is for IBM and other name brands, the market is wide open for anyone to sell clones at any price. Garage dealers can be found by word-of-mouth or in the classified section of the newspaper. Their adds in the classifieds look the same as those of clone dealers.

The different personalities and situations of the garage dealers make it hard to generalize about buying from them. Don't buy an 8088-based computer unless the garage dealer offers at least a one-year warranty. Your main question will then be whether or not they'll be able to honor it. The answer depends on three things: (1) the dealers' personal integrity, (2) whether or not they'll be around for a year, and (3) whether or not their supplier will be around to back them up. The volatility of the computer market makes it hard to tell who will still be in business tomorrow. Even large computer manufacturers go out of business, and large computer retail stores have been closing down recently, too. So buying from garage dealers is as secure or insecure a way to purchase a computer as any other.

Some advantages of buying a clone from a garage dealer could include: a more personalized service, better consultation, greater support, custom installation, etc. Because they work with virtually no overhead, it's possible for garage dealers to remain competitive and viable sources for an XT clone computer.

## Computer Shows and Swap Meets

Computer shows tend to be rather grandiose. They will frequently have not only product introductions and flashy exhibits, but seminars as well. The shows are typically held in big exhibition halls and will have both manufacturers and dealers exhibiting their wares. Computer swaps on the other hand are down-sized and only have local dealers selling their wares.

Computer shows and swaps are about the least expensive places to buy an XT clone. The prices come close to a dealer-cost level, which means that amazing bargains can be found. This is primarily because of fierce competition, with one booth next to another selling the same clones and clone accessories. There is typically a wide variety of parts available at both computer shows and swaps. This means that you have a wide selection from which to choose.

Buying at a show or swap can, however, be confusing since there are so many vendors and parts to choose from. For the first-time buyer, it is best to purchase an assembled-and-tested computer from one dealer. This way, if the system should fail, the buyer will know to whom to return it. I don't recommend purchasing parts from many dealers and assembling the system yourself. If you do wish to assemble the computer yourself, purchase at least the basic parts from one dealer, otherwise you may have warranty problems.

To determine what kind of person or company you are dealing with, get a price quote and ask if they will maintain that price after the show. If so, go to their place of business and check it out. Often dealers will lower their prices toward the end of a show. This is because they're anxious to sell, rather than repack and carry home their unsold wares. Be careful. Often, at the end of the show (or even from the beginning of a show), outdated or demo units that dealers don't want in their stores are unloaded on the unsuspecting customer. You should also be aware that dealers sometimes need quick cash, and may liquidate perfectly good inventory at a show, offering you some very good bargains.

To find the location and dates of computer shows and swap meets, look in local newspapers and especially in free local tabloid computer magazines. Appendix C of this book contains a list of show and swap promoters. You can call or write the one in your area for information on their next show.

*Figure 5.6*   Computer shows are a good place to find bargains

## Mail Order

Buying a computer by mail order is a "blindfold on" affair and
you may feel intimidated by the thought.  Nevertheless, the mail
order computer field has become big business in America. $2.1
billion worth of computer equipment was sold last year through
mail order companies in America, according to **Future Computing Inc.**, a Richardson, Texas research firm.  Obviously, a lot of
buyers are willing to trust mail order firms as legitimate and
trustworthy sources.

*Figure 5.7*    Computer mail order sales are mushrooming

Mail ordering a computer couldn't be simpler. You just call (usually a toll free number) or send in an order form, and the U.S. Mail or a parcel service company delivers a computer to your door within a week or two.

However, mail order is not for every buyer. Typically, it is more appropriate for the informed buyer who is already familiar with computers and computer prices. It is a very convenient way for a buyer (even a novice), who happens to live in some remote place like Death Valley, California, and has no way to get to a convenient computer outlet. For this buyer, ordering from a magazine advertisement is the only alternative.

In general, the basic advantage of buying a computer through the mail is price. Due to mail order firms having low overhead (due to no showroom, no sales staff, no repair shop), they can offer the consumer rock-bottom prices. Mail order firms also tend to handle high volume, which can further lower the price. Some mail order companies even do direct importing of parts and machines, and therefore, their wholesale costs are lower. These savings are typically passed on to the buyer. Even the so-called "garage dealers" cannot compete with these prices since they are too small to import parts themselves.

Other advantages to ordering a computer by mail include the mail order firm's wide selection of products. Many brands and types of parts and computers are available as well as software, accessories, computer books and more. You can shop from the comfort of your arm chair and enjoy delivery to your home without the hassle of going from computer store to computer store.

Nevertheless, there is an element of risk in buying through the mail; you do not always know what you are getting until it arrives. You may, for example, get an especially noisy disk drive, a poor keyboard, or a loud power supply that you could pre-test in a store and reject if it's not right.

Another potential disadvantage is that there are sometimes hidden costs. Two such possible costs are delivery charges and surcharges which are often applied to credit card purchases. Ask lots of questions when buying by mail order and make sure the firm has a toll-free technical hotline for help later in the event that you have a problem with your purchases.

The computer mail order business has gotten some bad press recently because several companies have gone out of business while leaving customers holding the bag with undelivered orders. When buying via mail order it is advisable to buy from a reputable firm. Check back issues of magazines for mail order houses' adds. The longer a specific firm has been advertising, the more reputable it is likely to be. It's also a good idea to call the Better Business Bureau office in the town where the firm is located to see if any complaints have been filed against them.

Buying with a credit card gives the buyer maximum leverage. If you pay with cash it can be difficult, if not impossible, to get your money back from a dealer in case of problems. If the merchandise were paid for with a credit card, you can ask for a credit memo and as a last resort, refuse payment.

When looking at a mail order ad, you will see many terms that may seem confusing. I went through some mail order adds and pulled out typically-used phrases. The following list comprises these phrases and their definitions:

## Add 3% for Visa and MasterCard

The percentage figure varies from company to company because the various credit card companies charge between 2.5 to 5% processing fee to their members. In turn, the mail order firm passes on this charge to the customer.

## Packing $3.50 per order

A charge is added to the cost of the order to cover the cost of packing. If you picked up the order directly, it would not be necessary to pay this fee.

## All orders are insured

While the order is being shipped from the mail order house to you, they insure it against any damage done by the shipper.

## No sales tax on out-of-state

This is one of the main advantages to mail order, no sales tax if the product is purchased out-of-state. If local sales tax is 6. 5% for example, you could save $130 on a $2000 purchase.

## All prices quoted FOB

FOB means Freight On Board, or that the price given does not include freight. Remember, the further you live from the company, the higher the shipping costs due to shippers charging by the mile or by zones.

## COD extra

COD stands for Cash On Delivery.  In other words, if you wish
to pay when the order arrives at your place, there will be an
"extra" charge by the shipper for this service.  The extra fee is
usually around $2 per order.

## All returns must have R.M.A. or they will be refused

R.M.A. stands for Return Merchandise Authorization.  Before
returning defective merchandise, you must call the mail order
house and state the reason for returning the item.  This is a
simple process, which involves the company issuing a number
that you write in large letters on the outside of the shipping box.

## 15% restocking charge

If returned merchandise doesn't have the RMA number, the mail
order house may impose a fee of 15%.

## Not responsible for typographical errors

If the magazine or printer makes a misprint of the advertisement,
the mail order house will not accept responsibility.

## 14-day returns on all hardware

This number can vary from no-returns to a 30-day return.  It
means that if you are not happy with the computer, you can send
it back for a full or partial refund within the mentioned time
span.

## Prices subject to change without notice. All items subject to availability

This statement is a disclaimer and done to protect the firm against the rapid change in prices. In this case the prices quoted in an ad can change (up or down) without the company notifying you. It is therefore important to verify price and availability of the product by phone before ordering.

*Figure 5.8*     "I'd like to order a computer with a technical support line and 14 days return privilege... and hold the COD"

## OEM

This is an abbreviation for Original Equipment Manufacturer. This means the company deals in large volume and will only sell their products to a firm who will place their own name on it and resell it.

## Personal check, allow 10 days to clear

In order to make sure the customer's check doesn't bounce, the mail order house will hold up the shipping for as long as 10 days. The time that a check is held varies according to the respective companies.

## Technical line available

In case a problem occurs with the product, a number can be called for technical support. It's especially nice of course, if it happens to be toll free.

# Section II

# Handbook

# CHAPTER 6

# UNDERSTANDING THE PARTS

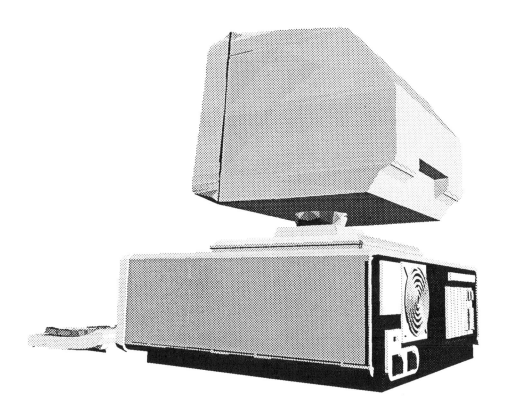

## Chapter Focus

This chapter explains in detail each of
the most common parts of the computer.
Each explanation is followed with
buying recommendations and a series of
tips for expanding the computer.

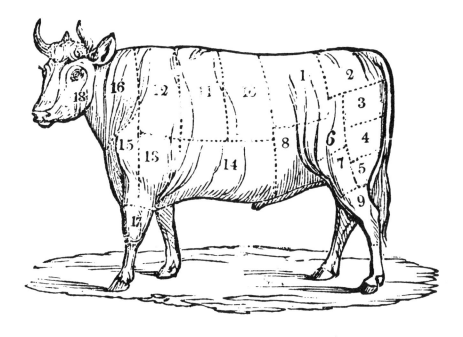

*Figure 6.1* The whole is made up of individual parts

＊＊＊＊＊

IT CAN BE quite helpful to learn something about the parts which make up the computer. This knowledge can be used for purchasing, expanding, upgrading, and troubleshooting your computer. A part merely refers to a complete stand-alone unit of the computer such as a keyboard, monitor, or expansion card. These parts all fit together with cables, screws, or edge connectors. There are only eight basic parts (sometimes called subassemblies) required to make up a functioning computer.

The eight parts required for a basic functioning XT clone consist of:

(1) chassis

(2) power supply

(3) motherboard

(4) floppy drive(s)

(5) floppy controller or multi I/O

(6) display card

(7) monitor

(8) keyboard

All other parts are optional and are used to enhance the capabilities of the computer. This chapter will cover some of the more popular add-on accessories. The most typical are:

(9) hard drives

(10) hard disk controller

(11) memory expansion cards

(12) modems

There are many manufacturers for each of the individual parts which go into the computer. For example, several different companies manufacture motherboards. Other companies make monitors, while others manufacture keyboards. Each has some variation in features and style. With so many different sources, you can expect a wide range of quality. Through careful shopping, you can be sure that only the best parts go into your computer. Whenever possible, I mention names (in **boldfaced** type) of manufactures and their products found to be reliable and of good quality. (The addresses of these companies can be found in Appendix A). All the thousands of potential parts cannot be examined here because of space restrictions and because there are so many new products coming onto the market on a weekly basis. Unless you have a highly specific application in mind, it is better to stay with the more common parts since they are widely available, easier to replace, and usually the least expensive.

*Figure 6.2*     "I've been out all day shopping for computer parts"

# Chassis

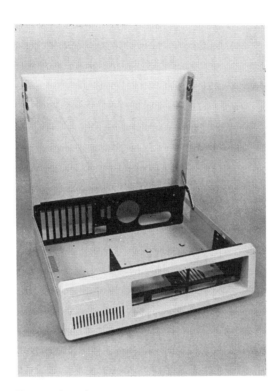

*Figure 6.3*    A flip-top chassis

The chassis is the frame within which the computer is housed. Most fall into one of two categories, the flip-top or AT slide-out type of chassis.

## Flip-Top Chassis

One very innovative characteristic of many XT clones is the flip-top chassis. This feature, above all else, helps to demystify the insides of the computer box for most people. With the flip-top chassis it is only a matter of pressing two buttons on each side of the chassis and lifting the lid to expose the interior of the computer. Most people's first response when they see what's inside is, "Is that all there is to a computer?" Then they start wondering what they're paying the high price for. The only other computer I know of on the market that has this easy access feature is the Apple IIe. Not all XT clones have this flip-top chassis, but I highly recommend it versus the kind of cabinet which must be unscrewed in the back to be opened. If you have a frequent impulse to tinker, do yourself a favor and get a flip-top case. With a flip top case, you can get to the motherboard and cards quickly and easily. (At least you can after you've moved all that stuff that accumulates on top of the computer). If you're often adding or subtracting equipment to your system, this kind of case is almost a necessity.

One problem with a flip-top chassis occurs if the computer is in a public area, it would be easy for someone to open the lid and quickly help themselves to your expansion cards. It's also not the kind of feature for someone who has small children. (There is a market waiting for someone to develop a flip-top lock for such situations). Another potential problem is that the flip-top chassis may not meet all FCC requirements and as a consequence has become more difficult to find these days.

### AT Look-Alike Chassis

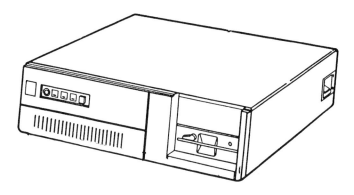

*Figure 6.4*    AT look-alike chassis

Many of the newer XT chassis have a keylock and indicator lights on the front panel and look like a smaller version of the AT chassis.  Be careful when buying this type of chassis because some are manufactured with bogus lights and locks.  The styling of this chassis looks good, but one disadvantage of this style is that only two drives are accessible from the front (as with the IBM AT).  It is therefore not possible to add a third internal floppy  drive.

## Buying Recommendations

The chassis is typically constructed of sheet metal which shields the circuitry against radio frequency interference.  It is important that heavy gauge metal be used.  Some chassis are made of light gauge metal and are not sturdy enough. This may cause the top of the chassis to sag under the weight of the monitor. Also, the chassis may bend or twist when moved or carried, resulting in possible damage to the motherboard. Whichever chassis you select, check that it has a good keylock assembly.

## Keylock Assembly

The keylock assembly consists of the keylock, switches, and indicator lights (sometimes called light emitting diodes LED's) on the front panel. Ideally, the assembly would be designed similar to the following drawing.

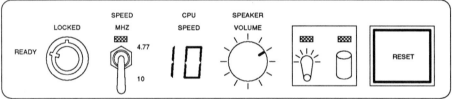

*Figure 6.5    An ideal keylock assembly*

**Keylock**    When the keylock is turned to the locked position, the keyboard becomes inoperable. This precaution is designed to prevent anyone from tampering with your program while the computer is left unattended.

**Power-on LED indicator**    This green light remains lit as long as the computer is on.

**Hard drive LED indicator**    This red light is on when the hard drive is being accessed.

**Turbo switch**    This hardware switch toggles between high and low speed, for example, 4.77 MHz to 8 or 10 MHz.

**Turbo LED indicator**    This light or digital readout states the speed at which the computer is operating.

**Reset switch**    Sometimes the computer may lock up. In this case, a reset switch allows the computer to be reset without the inconvenience of turning the entire system off.

**Speaker Volume control**    This control knob would allow the ability to turn down the volume of the speaker.

As of yet, I have not seen a computer with all these features on the front panel where they belong. The keylock assembly mentioned here is an ideal one because it has the important controls all at your finger tips. In the typical computer however, some of these switches may be found on the back panel or not at all.

# Expansion Tips

### Standing the Computer on its Side

A recent innovation in computer design has been the "tower design." With this design, the computer stands on its side on the floor rather than laying flat on a desk. This, of course, frees up a great deal of precious desk space. A low cost alternative to buying a computer with this design is to simply turn your standard XT computer on its side. Make sure the power switch is on top and that your computer will not fall over, rock or be kicked. (Rocking a computer while the hard disk is running can cause it to lose data or crash). A low cost stand can be purchased at many computer supply houses for about $30 or less.

# Power Supplies

*Figure 6.6*    A 150 watt power supply

The power supply converts the typical 110-volt house current into the various voltages required by the computer. Each subassembly draws some electricity which is measured in watts. The typical XT clone comes equipped with a 150 watt power supply. This is more than adequate for most needs. The reason for this is that computer technology is moving toward the use of more efficient chips, which require a fraction of the electrical current of previous chips. This means power supplies can be smaller and less costly. For example, IBM's PS/2 Models 30 use this new chip technology and require only a 70 watt power supply.

# Power Requirements in Watts

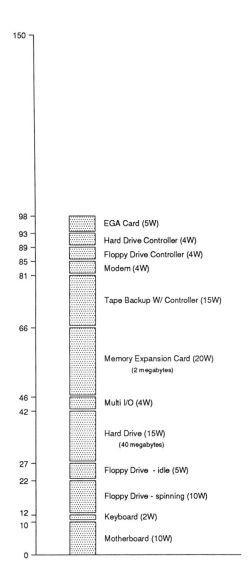

# Buying Recommendations

When buying a power supply (or shopping for a computer and comparing power supplies), check for the following features:

**Low noise level**    The most usual annoyance of a power supply is the fan. Some fans are quieter than others. Unfortunately, they all make some noise. Before purchasing a computer or power supply, check to make sure the fan is not excessively noisy.

**Initializing pulse**    If you buy a power supply and want to be prepared for a possible XT to AT/386 upgrade in the future, be sure it has the proper initializing pulse on pin 1. Many of the power supplies under 180 watts for the XT, do not have the proper initializing pulse and will not work with an AT/386 making the purchase of a new power supply (around $65) necessary.

**Automatic overload and open circuit shutdown**    Check to see if the power supply has "overload protect." If a short circuit or overload develops in the computer, the power supply will save itself from being damaged by automatically shutting off. This feature may save other components as well. The open circuit shutdown feature turns off the power supply in the event that an open circuit develops in the computer. This is yet another component-saving feature.

**Switchable voltage**    If you're planning to travel abroad with your computer, make sure the power supply can be switched from 110 to 220 volts to accommodate foreign voltages.

**UL approval**    Check that the power supply has been approved by Underwriter Laboratories. All approved devices contain a sticker with the UL name on it.

Skynet Electronics CO. (which is a Taiwanese manufacturer) offers a well-built, 150-watt power supply which will fit in an XT case and has the proper AT/386 initializing pulse. It is, therefore, an excellent choice for those who might upgrade to an AT or 386 computer in the future.

# Expansion Tips

### Replacing the Power Supply

It may be that your present power supply does not have enough wattage to support all the expansion features you would like to add, or maybe that the fan is too loud and annoying. In either case, it is an easy matter to replace the power supply with a more powerful or quieter one. Use the instructions in Chapter Seven and Eight for actual removal and replacement of the power supply.

### Adding a Y Connector.

The typical power supply has four power connectors which connect to drives. If you add a fifth drive, you will need to add a special connector called a "Y connector." This Y connector fits into an existing connector and branches into two other connectors. Y connectors are available at electronics stores as well as most computer swap meets.

## Adding a Surge Protector

Variations in electrical power (such as spikes and surges) can damage your computer. For this reason be sure to use a surge protector on your computer. There are many kinds available. The cheaper ones use a "gemov voltage clamp" and are available for $30 or less; they offer protection only against the worst voltage irregularities. The more expensive surge protectors use a built-in AC filter and will do a much better job of stabilizing the electrical current to the computer. If you have very unstable electrical current you definitely should use the better surge protector; if your electrical voltage is quite stable, a less expensive one is probably adequate. Also of great convenience are the surge protectors which sit on top of the computer and under the monitor. They have a series of on/off switches in the front for the computer, monitor, printer, external modem, lamp, etc. This type are handy because they place all the electrical power controls conveniently at your finger tips.

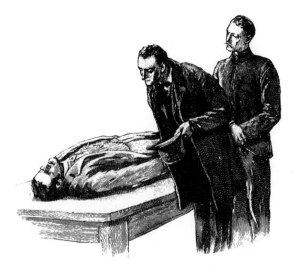

*Figure 6.8*     "He forgot to turn the power off before adding an expansion card"

# Motherboards

*Figure 6.9*    An original IBM XT motherboard

The motherboard is the central subassembly in the computer. It consists of a flat, printed-circuit board on which is mounted a variety of chips and a few other components. The motherboard contains the 8088 CPU, the support circuitry, the socket for the 8087 math coprocessor, the BIOS chip, several rows of memory chips, and 8 expansion slots. These components will be discussed in more detail in the following pages.

*Figure 6.10*    An XT clone motherboard

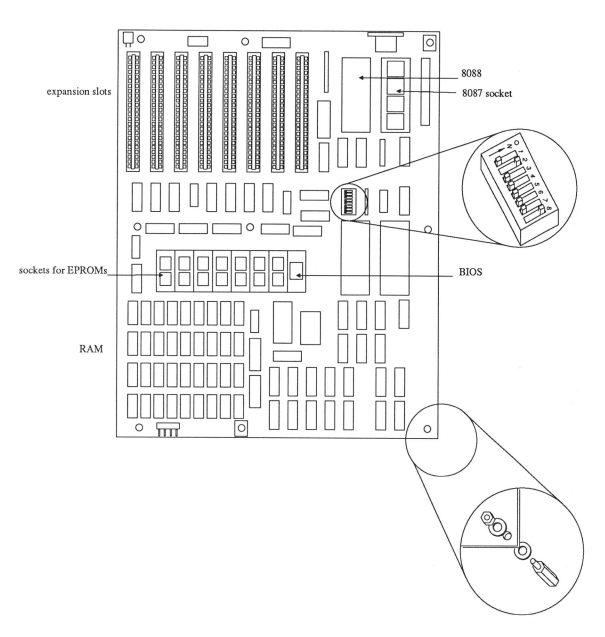

*Figure 6.11* The parts of the motherboard

## 8088

*Figure 6.12*    An 8088 chip

The 8088 is the central processing unit (CPU) designed by **Intel Corporation** of Santa Clara, CA.  This is the CPU or "brain" of the XT computer and determine the nature the computer.  Physically, the 8088 is a rectangular chip with 40 pins and fits into a socket on the motherboard.  It is designed for easy removal. This CPU can address up to 1024 K of memory, and works with the MS/PC-DOS operating system.  This microprocessor has a 16-bit internal data path but communicates with the outside world via an 8-bits data path.  (The 8086, a sister chip, has a 16-bit internal architecture and a 16-bit data path).  There are several versions of this chip, they are the:

- 8088, which is rated at 4.77 MHz

- 8088-2, which is rated at 8 MHz

- 8088-1, which is rated at 10 MHz.

## V-20 chip

*Figure 6.13*   A V-20 chip

The V-20 from **NEC** is the Japanese equivalent of the **Intel** 8088. The V-20 contains almost twice the amount of transistors as the original 8088. It is fully software and hardware compatible with its Intel counterpart, but performs between 10 to 25 percent faster due to its clever redesign. It is a CMOS device as opposed to the older NMOS technology. The net advantage is a much lower power drain (about 20 per cent that of the 8088). The device runs cool and should therefore last forever. All programs which will operate with the 8088 will run with the V-20. The price of this chip depend on the speed rating, from about $8 for a 5 MHz version to about $10 for the 10 Mhz unit.

## 8087 Math Coprocessor

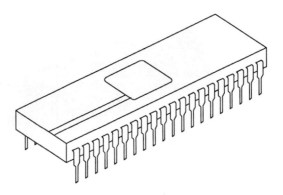

*Figure 6.14*    An 8087 math coprocessor

On all XT clones, a socket is left empty on the motherboard for the 8087 math coprocessor. The 8087 is similar in appearance to the 8088 CPU. It is a rectangular 40-pin chip which can significantly speed up (as much as 10 times) the processing of large, time-consuming mathematical calculations. This chip is specially designed to do floating point arithmetic extremely fast. Software, however, must be specifically written to use it. Some programs that are designed to take advantage of this chip are math intensive spreadsheets and Computer Aided Design (CAD) programs.

## Read Only Memory (ROM)

*Figure 6.15*    ROM chip

ROM is a type of memory chip. It contains data which the computer can read but not alter. Software is often embedded in ROM. IBM elected to store the programming language BASIC into a ROM chip on the PC, XT and AT. Any piece of software can be placed into a ROM. For example, if your favorite word processing program were placed in ROM, you would not need to load it from the hard or floppy drive. To get a new update of the program, you would have the inconvenience of changing chips. For this reason (among others), software is not often placed into ROM. Usually, two to six empty sockets are found on the XT clone motherboard for custom ROM chips.

## Basic Input/Output System (BIOS)

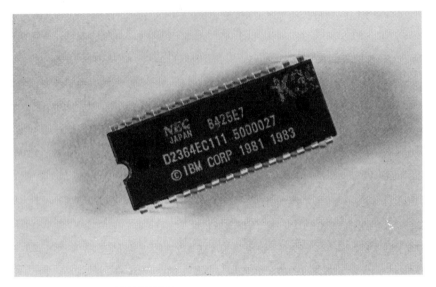

*Figure 6.16*    An IBM XT BIOS

One chip, the BIOS, is the critical part which determines
software compatibility with IBM.  In the IBM XT, the BIOS is
contained in one chip.  The BIOS is actually the code within a
chip called an EPROM (Erasable Programmable Read-Only
Memory).  This EPROM can be compared to a cassette tape -
any software program may be copied onto it.  It is also possible
to erase its contents using ultraviolet light and recopy a new
program onto it.  In other words the BIOS is the (erasable)
program contained in the chip.  This program controls the operations of the computer and peripherals.

IBM zealously guarded its BIOS and wouldn't sell it to
anyone unless they purchased IBM's whole computer.  If IBM
would have sold their BIOS separately, it could have been added
to an XT clone and the resulting product would literally have

*Figure 6.17* An XT clone BIOS

been an IBM XT. It is almost as easy to make copies of EPROM's as it is to make copies of cassette tapes or floppy disks. The process takes three or four minutes with a device known as an EPROM burner. EPROM burners are available for under $100 and may also be rented at some computer parts stores. The cost of a blank EPROM and the rental of a burner is under $15. Burning the EPROM only involves placing the chip to be copied into one socket and a blank EPROM into the socket next to it. Then the EPROM burner copies the contents of the original onto the blank EPROM by burning new pathways through the silicon. Under U.S. copyright law, it is illegal to do this, so what clone manufacturers have done is write their own BIOS as close as legally possible to IBM's. There are many different legal BIOSs available. All are fairly compatible with IBM's, although some are better than others.

## Random Access Memory (RAM)

*Figure 6.18*    RAM chips

RAM consists of computer chips which store information. They are installed in rows (called "banks") of nine on the motherboard. Only 8 chips per row are used to store data while the 9th is used for parity checking. Data transfer between the CPU and RAM occurs at the fastest possible rate since it involves no moving parts as do hard and floppy disk drives.

There are two kinds of RAM available.

**Dynamic Random-Access Memory (DRAM)** Dynamic RAM is the type of memory most often used. It is "volatile," meaning that it will retain data only as long as the computer is turned on. Any loss of power (even a momentary flicker in electricity) and the data in RAM will vanish.

**Static Random-Access Memory (SRAM)** Static RAM is not a very common form of memory because it is very expensive. It has the advantage however, of being able to retain data with the use of a battery.

**RAM Speed** The speed of RAM chips is measured in nanoseconds (ns); one nanosecond equals a billionth of a second. The speed of RAM installed into the computer must match with the computer's speed. If improper speeds are used, the overall operation of the computer will be slowed or the entire system may lock up. The following lists the speed of RAM chips needed with each CPU speed;

- 4.77 MHz CPU needs 200 ns RAM chips

- 8 MHz CPU needs 150 ns RAM chips

- 10 MHz CPU needs 120 ns RAM chips

**RAM Capacity** There are different memory capacities for RAM chips, these are; 16 kilobit, 64 kilobit, 256 kilobit, and 1 Megabit. The 1 megabit chips are still expensive, so usually 256 and 64 kilobit chips are used in most computers. Typically there are two "banks" (rows) of the 256 K and two banks of 64 K chips with a combined capacity of 640 K on the motherboard.

## How to Decipher RAM Chips

The size and speed of the RAM chip is printed on the top of each chip. Following is a drawing of a RAM chip and an explanation of how to read the chip.

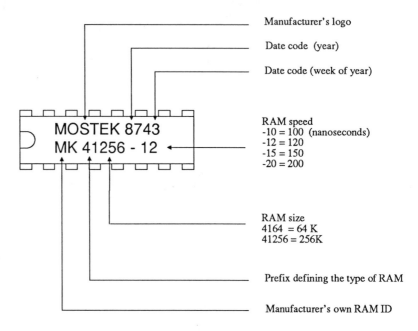

*Figure 6.19*    How to read a RAM chip

## Expansion Slots

*Figure 6.20*    Eight expansion slots

Expansion slots are connectors on the motherboard into which expansion cards can fit. Usually 8 of these slots can be found on the XT type motherboard and 6 of these slots can accept full length expansion cards while two can accept only short or half length cards because the drives are in the way.

## Bus

The bus connects the expansion slots and chips on the motherboard. The bus is important because it sets the standard for connecting add-on cards to the computer. If the bus and cards have different connectors, then they won't work together. As mentioned, there are two bus types available; the 8-bit XT/16-bit AT bus and the other is the PS/2 series Micro Channel bus used in the IBM PS/2 lines of 286 and 386 computers.

## Buying Recommendations

Many different brands of motherboards exist.

**Turbo Boards**    Motherboards are available with faster speeds than the IBM XT's 4.77 MHz.  These turbo boards are the most popular now because their price has fallen to where they are only slightly more expensive than regular 4.77 MHz boards.  Speeds for turbo boards are typically 8, 10, or even 12 MHz.  If you purchase a turbo board, it's best to look for the 8 or 10 MHz models which are the most common and reliable.  Turbo boards can be switched between 4.77 MHz and their faster speed either with software or hardware.

**4-Layer Motherboard**    The four layer motherboard's circuitry is better insulated than that on a standard 2-layer mother board.  Two layer boards have all their circuits in one layer, while the 4 layer boards have a layer of circuitry, then a layer of insulating material and then another layer of circuitry.  This has as its major benefit reduced electronic noise between circuits, which could cause parity errors.  This type of motherboard may be advisable for someone with high volumes of data to process at a low error tolerance level.  The main difficulty with this sort of board is that, if it should crack, it is virtually impossible to repair.  For an average user the added expense of this board and its potential high replacement cost don't justify it.

**Super Motherboard**    The super motherboard has the floppy disk controller, one parallel, two serial ports, and a clock/calendar all directly on the board.  At the present time, it is cheaper to purchase a regular turbo motherboard with a multi I/O (Input/Output) card, which contains the added features, than to buy a super board.  This is probably due to the large quantities of regular boards being manufactured; if the super boards start selling in greater quantities their prices may fall and they may become more popular.

**Short or half sized motherboard**     The circuitry of chips is continuously being integrated into fewer and fewer chips.  The latest XT clone motherboards have integrated the 30 or so chips that it took to make a motherboard into one chip!  These boards therefore contain only the 8088, a socket for the 8087, a BIOS, a keyboard BIOS, and one single chip besides the RAM.  This draws less power and gives off less heat.  The first mini motherboards based on the **Faraday** single chip had, unfortunately, some limitations.  They didn't support LEDs or the keylock and wouldn't boot up in turbo mode. In addition to these design problems, the failure rate was close to 50%.  If these bugs get worked out, these motherboards should become quite popular.

**Which motherboard to purchase?**     **DTK** makes far and away the most and lowest cost XT clone motherboards. 10 MHz turbo boards from **DTK** seem to be the most popular today and the most available.  The price of such a board without memory chips (0K) is around $80 to $90.

# Expansion Tips

### Adding an 8087 Math Coprocessor

When purchasing a 8087 math coprocessor, remember that its speed does not have to exactly match the computer's clock rate because it only operates at 3/4 the speed of the computer. To install the chip merely plug it into the socket with the halfmoon orientation notch facing the same direction as all the other chips. Remember, it is necessary to change the # 2 dip switch on the motherboard after installing the math coprocessor.

### Adding RAM

When purchasing RAM to add to the motherboard, make sure it is the correct speed (see the list on page 201). Follow the instructions in Chapter 7 for the actual installation. Also, remember to change the # 3 and # 4 DIP switches on the motherboard according to the amount of memory installed.

### Adding a New BIOS

It is possible that you may come across a program that does not work with your specific BIOS or you may just want to upgrade to the latest BIOS release, which may be faster. In this case, it is an easy matter to pull out the chip and replace it with a new one. A new BIOS may cost from $10 to $30 and is usually available from clone dealers. The dealer from whom you initially purchased your computer may upgrade your old BIOS with the latest release at no charge. Use the instructions in Chapter Seven for replacing the BIOS. Some Good BIOSs are:

*DTK/ERSO BIOS* made by **DataTech** in Taiwan. This BIOS is found in all **DTK** products and is adequate although not very fast.

*Phoenix BIOS* made by **Phoenix Technology** from Massachusetts. This is one of the most popular and widely used in IBM compatible type computers. It is much faster than the **ERSO** BIOS.

*Award BIOS* made by **Award Software** in Los Gatos, California. A favorite of mine.

*AMI BIOS* made by **American Megatrends, Inc**. in Atlanta, Georgia is also a very good product.

## Adding a V-20 Chip

Replacing the 8088 central processing unit with a V-20 chip will give your computer between a 10 and 20 per cent speed increase depending on the software. Adding the chip is very straight forward. Just pull out the old 8088. Ideally you would use a chip puller which is designed for the job. However, a screw driver can be used to pry the chip out. Once the 8088 is removed, carefully plug in the V-20 chip and be careful not to bend any pins. It is not required to change any jumpers or DIP switches after the process is completed.

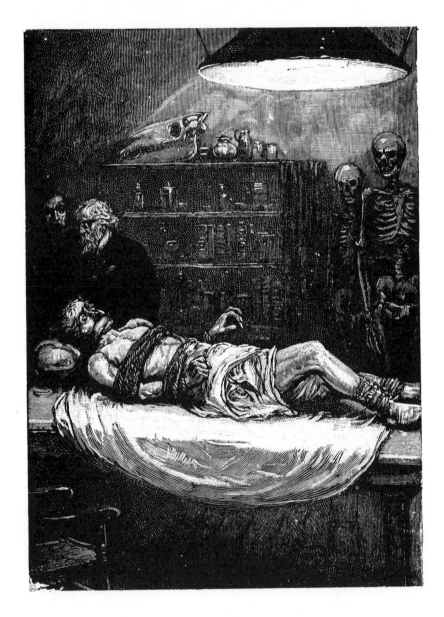

*Figure 6.21*    Using a poor quality BIOS can be a terrifying experence

# Floppy Disk Drives

*Figure 6.22*    A 3 1/2 inch and 5 1/4 inch floppy drive and a 3 1/2 inch floppy disk
(*Courtesy* **Fujitsu America, Inc.**)

Floppy disk drives can be likened to cassette recorders, both disk drives and cassette recorders save information in a magnetic medium. The information is stored on a removable and easily transportable floppy disk. Floppy drives come in a variety of shapes, sizes, and capacities. The trend is towards smaller disks, which paradoxically hold larger amounts of data.

There are four common types of floppy drives to choose from, each has a different capacity to store data. They are:

- 5 1/4 inch 360 K drives

- 5 1/4 inch 1.2 megabyte drives

- 3 1/2 inch 720 K drives

- 3 1/2 inch 1.44 megabyte drives.

### 360 K, 5 1/4 Inch Drive

The most common floppy drive is the 5 1/4 inch. It is referred to as a 5 1/4 inch drive because that is the size of the floppy disks it accepts. Because it is the most common drive, the majority of software companies offer their master disks in this format.

### 1.2 Megabyte, 5 1/4 Inch Drive

The 1.2 Megabyte floppy drive is also referred to as a "high density 5 1/4 inch drive"; this is because it packs up to 1.2 megabytes of data on special 5 1/4 inch floppy disks. The 1.2 megabyte drive can read data from a 360 K disk but will not write reliably to the 360 K disk. Typically, an IBM XT, compatible, or clone can not be fitted with one of these drives because the controller card will not support them. This kind of floppy drive will only run on an XT with the use of a special (and a bit more expensive) controller card.

### 720 K, 3 1/2 Inch Micro Floppy Drive

The smaller 3 1/2 inch floppy drive format (initially released by **Sony** and incorporated in the **Apple** *Macintosh*) is slowly taking over from the old 5 1/4 inch drive format. The 3 1/2 inch drives are superior to the 5 1/4 inch floppy drives. They are compact, quieter, more reliable, require less power (allowing the power supply to be smaller), and offer a higher data storage capacity. They use 3 1/2 inch floppy disks which are enclosed in a nondeformable, flat plastic jacket. These disks are better protected than the flimsy 5 1/4 inch disks and are easier to carry, fitting conveniently into a shirt pocket. You can even set your coffee cup on them without harm (a major advantage).

As of April 1987, IBM has opted to incorporate the micro floppy format on its entire PS/2 series. With IBM's endorsement, the 3 1/2 inch floppy drive is becoming the industry standard. These drives require DOS 3.2 or above and can hold 720 K of information.

### 1.44 Megabyte 3 1/2 Inch Micro Floppy

IBM was the first to announce the 1.44 Megabyte micro floppy. It is the same size as the 720 K drives but packs more data on special high density floppy disks. These drive typically will not work on the XT clone without the use of special floppy controllers. Besides that, these drives require DOS 3.3.

### Future Technology

The capacity of drives continues to increase. **Kodak** has already announced a 6.6 megabyte micro floppy and **Toshiba** talks about a 10 megabyte micro floppy drive. It looks, therefore, as though the 1.44 megabytes drives will still not be the last word in high storage capacity.

# Buying Recommendations

As mentioned, there is a transition taking place now from the
5 1/4 inch to the 3 1/2 inch drives.  Unfortunately, this transition
is turning out to be rather awkward. For example, if you install
only 3 1/2 inch drives you will be faced with the problem of not
being able to use 5 1/4 inch disks from your friends.  The best
solution therefore is to use one 3 1/2 inch 720 K and one 5 1/4
inch 360 K drive.  This allows you to read both types of disks.

*Figure 6.23*    A 5 1/4 inch and 3 1/2 inch floppy diskette

For 5 1/4 inch drives, some good quality brands are made by **Teac, Fujitsu,** and **Toshiba.**

For 3 1/2 inch micro floppies, some good drives are made by **Toshiba, Sony, Teac, Fujitsu**, and **Epson.** When purchasing the drive separately, be sure they come with the proper connectors and mounting brackets.

Whichever drives you choose, be sure that they are quiet. Noisy drives are often badly built. Check this by copying a program from one drive to the next and running programs that access the drive frequently. When purchasing drives separately, be sure to ask about the proper jumper settings for use with the XT.

# Expansion Tips

### How to Install 3 1/2 Inch Floppy Drives

If you have an XT with only 5 1/4 inch drives, you may wish to retrofit it with the smaller micro floppy drive. If you wish to add a 720 K floppy no special controller is required. First, be sure that when you purchase the drive, you get the needed documentation on how to assemble the drive and brackets (if it does not come assembled already). It is an easy matter to install a new drive into the computer. There are only a few screws holding the drive in place and two connectors to undo. For the actual physical installation of the drive, refer to chapter 7 on assembling the computer. Be sure you are using DOS 3.20 or above and have a BIOS which supports the drive. In order to use the 3 1/2 inch drive, it may be necessary to add a line in the computer's CONFIG.SYS file. The line to add is:

```
DRIVPARM=/D:1/F:2
```

This "undocumented" command lets you address and format the drive directly as B.

The following command let's you address the drive directly as drive A.

```
DRIVPARM=/D:0/F:2
```

# Floppy Controllers or Multi I/O Cards

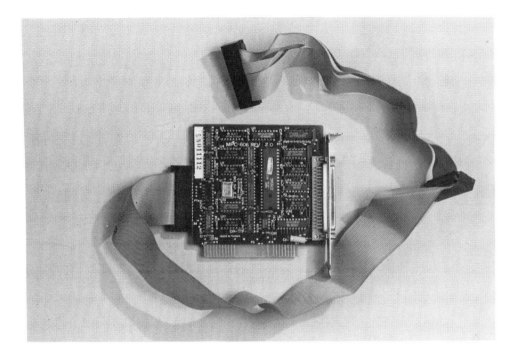

*Figure 6.24*    A floppy controller

Every accessory (such as a floppy disk drive, hard disk, monitor, etc.) needs an interface card; this card is also referred to as "plug-in board," "expansion card," or "controller." For floppy drives, the interface card is referred to as a floppy disk controller. The floppy controller often can be had as a separate card. Most controllers can drive up to four floppy drives, but few people use more than two floppy drives so this feature is unimportant. When buying the card, remember to purchase the cable which is needed to connect the drives to the floppy controller.

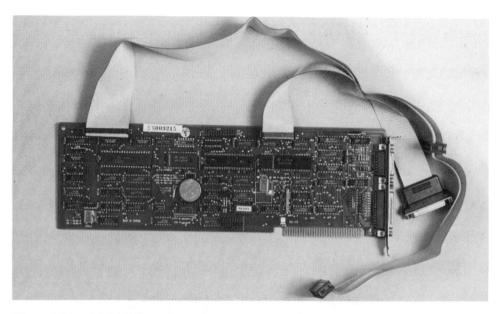

*Figure 6.25*    A Multi I/O card

If you will need a serial port for an external modem or mouse, a parallel port for your printer, a game port for a joy stick, and/or a battery-backed clock and calendar, you should have a Multi I/O card.  This card has all these features plus a floppy controller, all on one card.  Its price is not high when you consider all the extra features you are getting.  This single card also saves a couple of expansion slots which you can use in the future.

## Buying Recommendations

For the best value, purchase a Multi I/O card instead of only a floppy controller.  When purchasing a computer, (especially a very low priced one) ask if the computer contains a Multi I/O card.  Often, on the very low priced clones, they come with only a floppy controller.  Then, if you want a Multi I/O card, the dealer may charge a lot for it. The price difference between a floppy controller and a Multi I/O card is often only about 40 to 50 dollars.

# Expansion Tips

### Adding 2 More Drives

If you are using a single card floppy controller, it will may be able to support up to four drives. It is then possible to have two 3 1/2 inch drives and two 5 1/4 inch drives installed. Two drives connect internally to the edge connector on the card while the other two connect via the female 37 pin connector on the back of the card. It will be necessary to attach a ribbon cable to the outside connectors and feed it back into the computer through one of the openings in the back of the computer. It is required to use the DRIVER.SYS command to access drives three and four. Also DIP switches # 7 and # 8 must be set accordingly. If all this sounds confusing, it is. For a more detailed explanation and a diagram, see the section in Chapter Seven regarding installation of floppy drives. Also see the table in Chapter Seven page 283.

# Display Cards

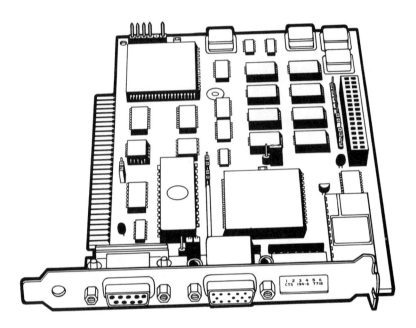

*Figure 6.26*    A VGA display card  (*Courtesy* **Video Seven, Inc.**)

Every monitor needs a card to control its operation.  This card is
referred to as a display or graphics card.  At this point in time,
display cards are one of the most confusing parts of the computer
because they are rapidly developing, thereby offering a wide
variety of choices to the buyer.  I've found that even computer
dealers are perplexed by all the choices.

A monitor and display card work in conjunction with each
other.  That is to say that a certain type of display card will only
work with a certain type of monitor.  The following chart lists
the eight major types of display cards and shows the monitors
that each group can support.  (Monitors will be covered separately under the MONITORS section of this chapter).

| Display Card | Type of Monitor |
|---|---|
| Monochrome Graphics Adapter (MGA) | TTL, Multiscan |
| Color Graphics Adapter (CGA) | Composite, RGB, EGA, Multiscan |
| Enhanced Graphics Adapter (EGA) | EGA, Multiscan |
| Professional Graphics Adapter (PGA) | PGA, Multiscan |
| Video Graphics Array (VGA) | VGA, Multiscan |
| Combination Cards | Various combinations |
| Super High Resolution Card | Super High Resolution Monitors |

The following time line shows the rapid development of new graphics standards.

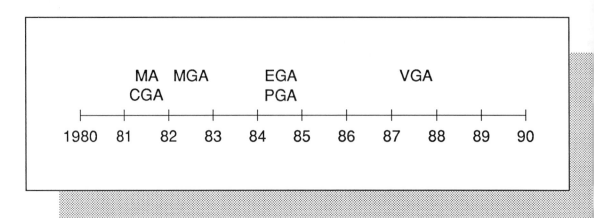

*Figure 6.27*    Timeline of the release of new video standards

## The Different Display Cards.

**Monochrome Adapter (MA)**    The monochrome adapter card was IBM's initial offering with the PC. The MA card drives a TTL as well as most multiscan monitors. This card should definitely be avoided because it cannot handle graphics, is over-priced and is quite obsolete.

**Monochrome Graphics Adapter (MGA)**    A small start up firm in Berkeley, CA called *Hercules Technology* took some of IBM's thunder away by adding graphics capabilities to IBM's monochrome adapter card, thereby creating a new standard with its *Hercules Graphics Card (HGC)*. Taiwanese manufacturers have in turn grabbed some of Hercules' thunder by making low cost clones of this card. The generic name sometimes used for these cards is *Monochrome Graphic Adapter (MGA).*

Parts for the Hercules card are all off-the-shelf, and Hercules only has a copyright on its manual and software which are needed to configure the computer. Hercules has been fighting an uphill battle against the clone makers. The early clones, made for use with Hercules software, were obviously illegal copies, right down to their photocopied Hercules manuals. The clone makers have now rewritten the configuration code and have stopped using the Hercules manual (this change came only after Hercules had taken several clone dealers to court).

**Color Graphics Adapter (CGA)**    CGA was IBM's first color standard and was released with the IBM PC. This card was used in conjunction with a "RGB" monitor. Even though there is a great deal of software available for the color graphics card and the card is inexpensive, I would advise against this type of card because of its very limited resolution. This standard has already been bypassed by other graphics standards.

**Enhanced Graphics Adapter (EGA)**    EGA was IBM's answer to the years of criticism of their mediocre CGA; EGA in fact, has now become the most popular card for color graphics. The card, either from IBM or one of its clones, is capable of running software written either for CGA, MA, or for (of course) EGA on either an RGB, EGA, or multiscan type of monitor.

**Professional Graphics Adapter (PGA)**    The quality of the image with EGA was still not high enough for many professional applications; so, in 1985, IBM offered the Professional Graphics Adapter (PGA) card and monitor. This card never really caught on with its intended market, the reason being that professionals who needed super high resolution displays have bypassed PGA for even higher quality cards and monitors.

**Video Graphics Array (VGA)**    VGA is IBM's latest offering in the color graphics display market. It was released with

IBM's new PS/2 series of computer in April of 1987. Previously, every time IBM has brought out a new display card, it has been quickly copied and offered at a lower price by clone makers. This, of course, has resulted in lost sales and profits for IBM. IBM used a new marketing strategy when it offered the VGA. Instead of placing the VGA on a card, it was integrated into one chip and soldered directly onto the motherboard. When purchasing a PS/2 computer, you must therefore take (and pay heavily for) IBM's display adapter.

VGA will surely become popular because it allows 265 simultaneous colors (out of a pallet of 256,000) to be displayed at one time and has a high resolution for text. VGA has further advantages in that it paints the screen faster and is, therefore, better for graphics-oriented programs such as the OS/2. VGA clone cards are readily available but the prices are still quite high. These two drawbacks should be quickly resolved as more companies offer clone cards and intense competition brings the price down to the level of EGA cards.

**MCGA**    MCGA stands for Multi-Color Graphics Array. IBM seems to have taken a great leap sideways with this technology. It offers no real technical or economic advantage over any other graphic standard. This display adapter is built into IBM's PS/2 model 30 and is a subset of VGA. MCGA can only be used with one of IBM's new analog monitors. At present, there is no independent developer of MCGA cards. With other more powerful standards developing (VGA), it is unlikely that any manufacturers will bother to produce MCGA cards.

**Combination cards**    One of the most clever developments with display cards is combination cards which combine several types of display adapters into one card and offer increased resolution.

The first generation of these cards was offered by Video-7, with the *Vega Deluxe*. It combines CGA, MGA, EGA, into one card. The market is now full of these types of cards which offer varying combinations of display possibilities.

The second generation of cards added an auto switching feature. These cards sense what monitor the software requires and automatically switch to the correct mode without the user needing to invoke a utility command. This generation of card also started offering the resolution of EGA and even up to and beyond PGA. Software or special "drivers", however, must be specially written to take advantage of the higher resolution. All cards which offer resolution beyond EGA also need a multiscan monitor.

The third generation improves on the previous ones that are available by claiming to run any software on any monitor. While it is a great concept, they seem to be flawed; they either create a noticeable flicker or don't work at all with some software. These cards are, therefore, not totally reliable.

The fourth generation of cards are the extended VGA cards. They go above the resolution of IBM's VGA and will support a resolution of 800 by 600, which is the maximum that most multi-scanning monitors can handle.

**Super High Resolution Cards**    The super high-resolution cards are custom-designed to go together as a set with a super high resolution monitor. They are designed for the professional market such as CAD or desktop publishing.

## Future Developments

Fancy colors and graphics require powerful processing
capabilities. The OS/2 operating system allows for greater
memory and therefore will also allow for display cards capable
of many more colors and higher resolution. New graphics
processors are also being developed which assist with the time
consuming task of processing graphic images. These developments mean that display cards and monitors will continue to improve and eventually place the graphic capabilities which are
now reserved for professional workstations on the average
person's desk.

*Figure 6.28*    "For your situation I'd recommend you buy a low cost EGA card now and that
you upgrade to VGA later when the cost comes down."

# Buying Recommendations

❏ If the computer is used primarily for text and simple graphics, I recommend a monochrome graphics card. These cards are available for as little as $50 and together with a TTL monitor are an inexpensive alternative. The clone cards do not generally have any recognizable brand names.

❏ If you want color, for the present, I recommend a low cost plain EGA clone card like the **Everex** *Micro Enhancer* or any of the low cost Taiwanese makes. The EGA combination cards are rather expensive and are only beginning to incorporate VGA. For that reason, I think it is better to hold off purchasing one of these. The present combination cards will be eclipsed by display cards which incorporate VGA as well as all the previous modes. If you want a combination card now anyway, the **Genoa** *SuperEGA* is commonly available at a competitive price.

   VGA cards are still expensive and not much software is available yet. Many manufacturers are getting into the VGA market, which should drive the price down rapidly. **Paradise Systems** makes the *VGA Plus Card* and the *VGA Professional Card*. These cards are both "BIOS" and "register" compatible with IBM and come with a two year compatibility guarantee and a three year warranty. They also support MGA, CGA, and EGA plus some extra modes.

❏ For professional use, such as CAD or desktop publishing, I highly recommend one of the super high resolution card and monitor sets. This alternative is discussed in greater detail under buying recommendations for monitors.

## Expansion Tips

### Adding a New Display Card

The task of upgrading your display card is not difficult. It merely involves opening up the computer and pulling out the old card. The new card then is replaced into the same expansion slot. For assistance with the actual process of opening the computer and installation of cards, check Chapter Seven. If you are changing from a monochrome to a color card, it is necessary to change DIP switch number five on the motherboard from "mono" to "color". Check your motherboard documentation to locate this set of dip switches or see the dipswitch table in Chapter Seven.

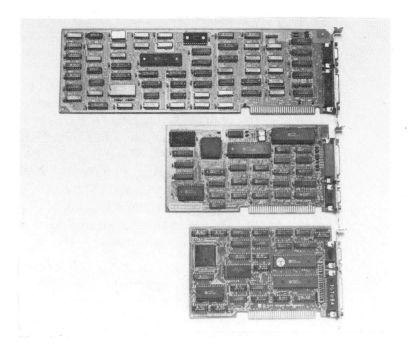

*Figure 6.29*    Display cards keep getting smaller

# Monitors

*Figure 6.30*    A monochrome monitor

You will probably be looking at your computer's monitor for extended periods of time. For this reason, it is important to find one which offers the maximum comfort for your eyes. The trend with monitors is toward ever higher resolution with increased numbers of color. There are quite a few different standards (or none at all, depending on how you look at it) from which to choose, and the choices continue to multiply.

There are nine major types of monitors available for use with an XT. The table below shows the types of monitors and their comparative features in terms of resolution, scanning rate, number of colors, and general cost.

# Type of Monitors

| | Monochrome Composite | Color Composite | Monochrome (TTL) | RGB (CGA) |
|---|---|---|---|---|
| **Resolution** | 640 by 200 | 640 by 200 | 720 by 350 | 640 by 350 |
| **Colors** | 1 | 4 | 1 | 4 |
| **Palette** | 1 | 4 | 1 | 16 |
| **Scanning Rate (In kilohertz)** | 15.75 | 15.75 | 18.40 | 15.75 |
| **Cost** | $40-80 | $140-200 | $70-160 | $250-400 |
| **Display** | Analog | Analog | Digital | Digital |
| **Year** | before 1980 | before 1980 | 1981 | 1981 |

## Definition of Terms

**Resolution**    Resolution refers to the quality of the image displayed on the monitor's screen and depends on the number of dots that are present; these dots are called pixels.  There are rows of pixels going across as well as down the screen.  The more pixels, the clearer and sharper the image, and higher the resolu-

| Commonly Used | | | | |
|---|---|---|---|---|
| **EGA** | **Multiscan** | **PGA** | **VGA** | **Super High** |
| 640 by 350 | 800 by 600 | 640 by 480 | 640 by 480 | 1200 by 800+ |
| 16 | unlimited | unlimited | 256 | Varies |
| 64 | unlimited | unlimited | 262,000 | Varies |
| 21.80 | 15.5 to 35 | 30 | 31.49 | 30 to 75 |
| $320-600 | $550-1000 | $550-1000 | $500-700 | $700-20,000 |
| Digital | Digital/Analog | Analog | Analog | Digital/Analog |
| 1984 | 1985 | 1984 | 1987 | before 1980 |

tion. A resolution of 640 by 350 means that there are 640 pixels displayed horizontally and 350 displayed vertically on the screen.

**Scanning rate**    The scanning rate is the amount of time it takes for an electron gun inside the monitor to draw a beam from one side of the screen to the other. The time is measured in kilohertz (KHz), or thousands of cycles per second. The faster the scanning rate, the more pixels that can be displayed on the screen, which results in a higher resolution.

**Color Palette**    The color palette is the full number of colors available.  It should be mentioned, however, that all the colors can not be displayed simultaneously.  To display many colors with high resolution, takes lots of memory.  Since memory is still in short supply, there is a choice to be made; either you have a large number of colors with limited resolution, or a few colors with higher resolution.

**Analog versus Digital**    There are two types of video signals, analog and digital.  The early microcomputers used low quality analog composite monitors.  Then, digital monitors became the standard; and now the trend is back to high quality analog monitors.  One  reason for the present trend toward analog monitors is that video graphics and computers are beginning to be linked.  To look lifelike, video needs many colors and shades of colors.  Analog is especially good at handling multitudes of colors and shades;  this is because analog works just like a volume control on your radio or television.  Using analog signals, you can change colors anywhere along the color spectrum, allowing minute variations on the color of red for example.  Digital, on the other hand, works in steps;  you can only change from one preset color to the next and cannot access the colors in between.

## The Types of Monitors

**Monochrome Composite**   The earliest computers used televisions as displays.  A typical TV, however, can only show about 40 characters on a line before text becomes unreadable.  To solve this problem and allow 80 characters per line, (the normal width of a page) the monochrome composite monitor was developed (monochrome meaning one color).  The resolution of this monitor was still extremely poor, and as a result, this type of monitor is no longer popular.

**Color composite**   The color composite monitor is similar to the monochrome composite except that it displays color.  Its resolution is even more limited than the monochrome composite monitor.  For that reason, it (along with the monochrome composite monitor)  has been thrown on the junk heap of technological obsolescence.

**Monochrome Display (TTL)**   When IBM introduced its PC in 1981, IBM also offered a new type of monitor.  This monitor came with a green screen and offered high resolution.  In advertisements you may see this type of monitor referred to as a TTL monochrome monitor because it uses transistor-transistor logic (TTL) circuitry.

Because of its high resolution, the TTL monitor quickly became the standard for word processing, spreadsheet, and other primarily text-oriented uses.  Presently, the majority of computers use TTL monitors because they are inexpensive and offer very good resolution.

**RGB (Red/Green/Blue)**   Another monitor IBM released with the PC was the Red/Green/Blue (RGB) monitor.  RGB refers to the 3 electron guns inside the monitor.  One fires one electron beam for red, another for green, and a third for blue.

These three colors together make up a palette of 16 possible colors.

The resolution on an RGB monitor is poor, resulting in fuzzy and eye-fatiguing text. This monitor has now become technologically out of date and is rarely seen any more.

**Enhanced Graphic Adapter (EGA) Monitor**    There were many complaints about the poor resolution of the RGB monitor.

*Figure 6.31*     A poor resolution monitor can ruin your eyesight

To address these complaints IBM introduced, in 1984, the Enhanced Graphic Adapter monitor.

EGA got off to a slow start because of IBM's typically high price and the initial lack of software support. However, manufacturers soon made clones of the EGA monitor. This, of course, has resulted in lower prices and increased software support. EGA is now very popular due to its color ability even though the resolution of text is only just of acceptable quality. The EGA's resolution is still not as sharp as that of a TTL monitor.

**Professional Graphics Adapter (PGA) Monitor**    The resolution of EGA was still not high enough for many professional applications, so in 1985, IBM offered the Professional Graphics Adapter (PGA) monitor. The price IBM asked for this monitor was quite exorbitant; for this reason (among others), PGA is essentially dead.

**Multiscan Monitors**  Moving from one generation of monitor and its corresponding display card has previously meant discarding the old monitor and purchasing a new one. For example; if you had purchased an RGB monitor and CGA card and then had upgraded to an EGA card, you would have had the added expense of purchasing an EGA monitor as well. This problem was somewhat resolved when **Nippon Electric Company (NEC)** brought out the first multiscan monitor that could be used with a wide variety of cards. It is a versatile type of monitor because it automatically synchronizes to the scanning rate of most display cards.

Many other companies are now releasing multiscan monitors and prices are steadily decreasing. These monitors are also known as "multi-displays" or as "multisyncs." **NEC** has a trade mark on the name *MultiSync*, however, because it was the first multiscan monitor. The word multisync has developed into one of the generic names for this type of monitor.

**IBM VGA Monitor**    In April 1987, IBM announced its new PS/2 series of computers, which came with a new analog monitor and display adapter called the Video Graphics Array (VGA). Clone makers have already started making IBM VGA clone monitors. Also, most multiscan monitors will work with the VGA card, so there is no shortage of third party monitors to be used with VGA cards.

This new standard opens up more new possibilities such as life-like video databases and interactive educational videos. For example, a real estate office can have a computerized database of color photos or even movies of the interiors of houses. Encyclopedias on disk (with high quality graphics and pictures) will also be a possibility. It is especially nice that a higher scanning rate is used, so that the monitors have less flicker and are therefore easier on the eyes.

**Super High Resolution (Full Page) Monitor**    Beyond the resolution of PGA and VGA is a non-standardized realm of resolution where each manufacturer more or less makes its own monitor and display card combination. Software must be written specifically to be used with each of these systems, or special "drivers" must be made available. There is no industry accepted term for this type of monitors. I refer to it as "super high resolution" or as "full page monitors" because they allow word processing and desktop-publishing software to show an entire page of 80 columns by 66 lines or more.

# Buying Recommendations

The question now becomes which of these different types of monitors to purchase?

- ❏ For text-oriented computer applications (such as word processing, spreadsheet, databases, and simple graphics capability), use a TTL monitor. They can be purchased for under $100 and cause less eye strain than larger color monitors. Some TTL displays at the low end are the **Mitsuba 510A,** and those made by **Casper**, and **Samsung**. Some better-made and higher-priced ones are **Quadram's** *Amberchrome*, **Princeton's Graphics** *Max 12,* and **Everex's** 14 " *Evervision*.

- ❏ Features to look for in TTL monitors include an amber (rather than green) phosphor screen. The green screen leaves distracting ghost-images behind when the display changes. From my own experience, amber is easier on the eyes for prolonged sessions in front of your monitor. It is also desirable to have a black anti-glare netting stretched across the screen, which cuts down reflections and increases contrast. Look at the monitor with a full page of text to see that columns of text are straight and properly centered within the screen; otherwise, it will be a constant annoyance if the text is, for example, crooked or curved.

- ❏ If you want color and wish to be prepared for the future, I highly recommend a multiscan monitor. That way, you'll be prepared for the VGA standard. You will also have the flexibility of using it with a wide variety of display cards and software. The **Sony** *Multiscan* is among the best of the multiscan monitors (it has the finest "dot pitch" in the industry). Some others are the **NEC** *Multi-Sync*, **Mitsubishi** *Diamond Scan* and the **Thomson** *Ultra Scan*. Whichever multi-scanning monitor you choose, double check that it takes an analog input and verify that it will accept VGA.

❏ If you are using CAD, desktop publishing, or other graphic intensive programs on a professional basis go with a super high resolution monitor. The savings (in ease of use and time saved) will quickly pay for their extra expense.

Some good monitors in this field include the *Wyse 700* from **Wyse Technology** of San Jose, CA. It has a resolution of 1200 by 800, and is attractively priced under $800. In the mid range, is the **CornerStone Technologies** *Vista 1800*, with a resolution of 1600 by 1280, it is priced around $2,000.

## Points to Check

Before choosing any monitor, it is a good idea to look at several models to get an idea of their different features. When shopping for any monitor, consider the following points:

❏ Check for flickering or blurring of the screen; you do this by turning the brightness to maximum. In the case where there is a color monitor, bring up some software which makes the screen white, and look at the image out of the corner of your eye. Your peripheral vision is most sensitive and you will see how much the screen flickers. You should especially look for a monitor with a steady image because a screen that flickers too much can cause headaches after prolonged viewing and is, therefore, very undesirable.

❑ Compare a few monitors to get an idea as to the clarity and sharpness of the images.

❑ Turn the contrast and brightness knobs and see if you can find a shading you are comfortable with.

❑ A built-in tilt and swivel is nice for adjusting the monitor to the most comfortable position.

❑ Make sure that the important control knobs are easily accessible. The best location is in front.

*Figure 6.32*   "My goodness! That looks almost as good as my VGA monitor"

# Expansion Tips

### Adding a New Monitor

You may want to upgrade a CGA to an EGA or multi-scanning monitor. This is easily done. The process entails adding a new display card if the old card does not support the type of monitor you wish to add. Change the DIP Switch information accordingly. See page 284.

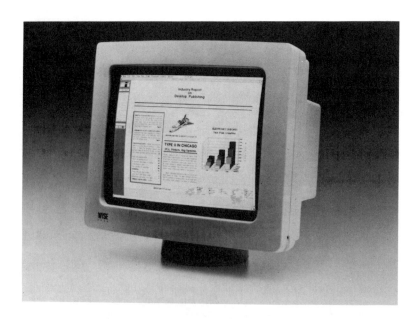

*Figure 6.33*    The *Wyse 700* super high resolution monitor (*Courtesy* **Wyse Technology**)

## Adding a Tilt Swivel Stand

The addition of a tilting swivel stand will go a long way towards making your computer more agreeable and fun to use. Having to tilt or twist your neck at an awkward angle to see the monitor is a sure way to promote backaches and neckaches. A stand that allows you to tilt and swivel the monitor can alleviate many of these problems. These stands can be inexpensively purchased through many computer magazines, at computer stores or at local computer swap meets.

## Glare Reducing Screens

Depending on the lighting situation where you work, reflective light glare can make it hard to see the screen. If neither the lighting nor the computer monitor can be moved to fix this problem, you might consider the purchase of a glare reduction screen. These are screens that fit over the computer monitor. They allow you to see the monitor screen, but scatter reflected light from external sources so that glare from external lights is no longer a problem. These can be purchased almost anywhere computer components are sold.

# Keyboards

*Figure 6.34*    AT Keyboard

Personal taste plays a large part in choosing a keyboard. Some
people like keys with a firm feel, some prefer mushy keys.
There are essentially two styles of keyboards for the XT. First is
the "AT layout," second is the "IBM enhanced layout." IBM
received a great deal of criticism for the keyboards it used on the
PC Jr., PC, and XT. When the AT was released they used a new
layout; IBM referred to it as the "AT layout." It has ten function
keys on the left, the standard keyboard layout with a large return
key, and cursor keys together with number keys on the right.
This layout still had a problem, especially for those working with
numbers because it is necessary to toggle between the cursor pad
and number pad. IBM then released a new layout with 101 keys,

which it now uses on all of its computers; it's referred to as the "IBM enhanced layout." This layout has 12 function keys across the top and a separate cursor and number pad. This design is rapidly becoming the industry standard.

### Keyboard Layout (QWERTY versus DVORAK)

The design of the standard keyboard layout stems from the early 1900s. At that time, typewriters' keys would jam up if the typist were to go too fast. The layout was, therefore, designed to slow down typists. This inefficient layout has been with us since that day. A new key layout has now been designed by a fellow named Dvorak, it is based on a simple notion of what is the most efficient key layout. If you have not yet learned to type, you may want to learn this new layout. It can double your typing speed. It is possible to change your existing keyboard to the DVORAK layout by simply invoking a DOS command. With the DOS disk in drive A, type "KEYBDV" to change the key layout. Stick-on tabs can then be used to relabel the keys.

## Buying Recommendations

Some keyboards work only with 8088-based computers while others work only on 286- or 386-based computers. Some keyboards are switchable so that they will work on either type of computer. These switchable keyboards are desirable, because they give the maximum flexibility and generally do not cost any more than the nonswitchable ones.

There are several features which are considered desirable in a keyboard. The features typically looked for are a long cord, raised bumps (or deep-dish caps) on the "F", "J" and numeric "5" keys (which act as homing keys to help orient touch-typists), and a feel you are comfortable with.

Since most computer makers are moving to the enhanced layout, it's probably best to go with this style since it is the emerging standard. A good quality and inexpensive keyboard is the *Maxi-switch* keyboard made by **The Maxi-switch Co**. It is highly recommended. This keyboard is switchable for use on either the XT or AT/386. The **Keytronics** is also very good.

*Figure 6.35*    Enhanced keyboard layout

# Expansion Tips

## Changing Keyboards

With the 101 key enhanced keyboard becoming the standard, you may find you would like to upgrade your old keyboard for a newer one. You may also be fed up with your existing keyboard which perhaps has an unpleasant feel. Upgrading is very simple, keyboards are generally under $100 so the upgrade is not expensive and only entails unplugging the old keyboard and plugging in the new. If the new keyboard is a switchable type and must be manually switched from AT to XT, make sure it is switched properly on the back of the keyboard. Some keyboards also allow the "Esc" and the "~" keys to be switched to whichever way is most convenient to you.

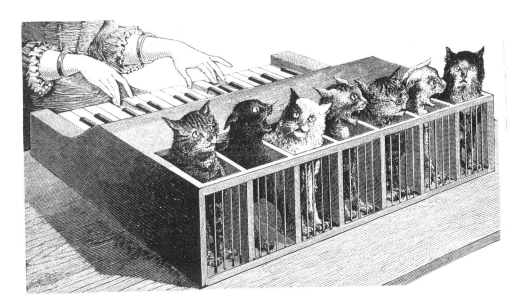

*Figure 6.36* ·Avoid nonstandard keyboards

# Hard Drives

*Figure 6.37*    ***Seagate ST 225***

A hard drive is essentially a sealed box with several rotating
metal platters inside. Information is stored on these rigid platters, just as it is on a floppy disk. Hard drives (also called
"Winchester drives") are quite fragile and care should always be
taken when handling one.

A hard disk drive is an enormous convenience. It allows for
large amounts of stored information to be quickly and easily accessed, without the bother of having to change from one floppy
disk to another. For example, if you are doing word processing,
you may have one floppy which holds the word processing system program, another for a spelling checker, another which holds
a thesaurus, and still another on which to record your data. To

switch from the word processor to the spelling checker and then to the thesaurus, you may have to swap several disks, some possibly more than once. With a hard disk, every function is directly accessible and your flow of work or creativity need not be broken with the petty chore of changing floppies.

## Hard Disk Features

**Physical size**    The most noticeable feature of a hard drive is its physical size. The largest ones are 5 1/4 inch full-height drives. This means they take up two drive bays in the computer. The next smaller drives are 5 1/4 inch, half-height and they take up only one drive bay. Another hard disk option is the new 3 1/2-inch hard disks. They are more compact, use the latest technology, draw less power and claim greater reliability than 5 1/4 inch hard drives. They are also more expensive, but prices are falling rapidly and should soon match the price of 5 1/4 inch hard drives and they will supersede them as the standard. IBM now uses them as standard equipment on its PS/2 line of computers.

**Hard Cards**    The "hard cards" are basically a 3 1/2-inch hard disk mounted together with the hard disk controller. This card is easy to install and fits into one of the expansion slots of the computer.

**Capacity**    With hard drives, capacity is measured in megabytes and refers to the amount of memory a hard disk can hold. Hard drives are available with anywhere from 5 to over 100 megabytes. 20 megabytes-and-up is the usual capacity of a hard drive in an XT.

**Speed (Access time)**    The speed of a hard drive refers to the amount of time it takes to access data. The average access time

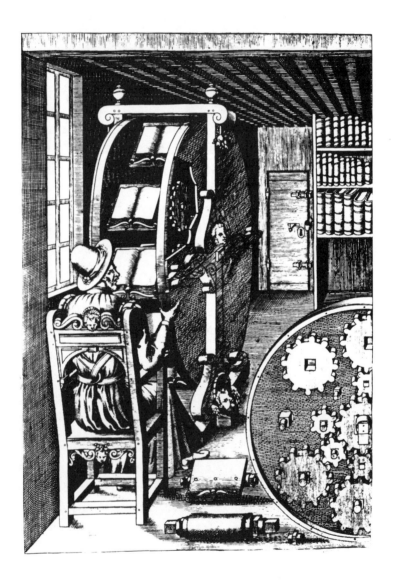

*Figure 6.38*    A 40 megabyte hard disk contains 20,000 pages of text

is expressed in milliseconds (ms). A typical speed for an XT is about 40 ms. 65 ms is considered slow; 28 ms is excellent; and 20 ms and below is considered unusually fast.

**Voice coil versus stepper motor**   Voice coil and stepper motor are the two head-positioning devices for Winchester drives. Voice-coil is very fast, precise, "self parking," and noise-less, but rather expensive. Stepper motor (while less expensive) is usually slower and noisier. It is noisy to the point that the read and write can be clearly heard.

*Figure 6.39*   "I used to be in business like you, until my hard disk crashed."

## Buying Recommendations

If you are purchasing a 8088-based machine, your primary reason is probably price. For that reason, it doesn't make sense to purchase an expensive fast hard drive, unless you plan to upgrade your computer in the near future. You'll probably want an inexpensive but reliable hard drive. Some further features to look for are:

&#9633; **Auto or self-park capability**    When not in use, the head assembly which reads and writes data on the disk goes automatically to a safe area near the center of the platter, hence the self or auto parking expression.

&#9633; **Good documentation**    Be sure to obtain good documentation with the drive. This includes information on how to format the drive and the proper drive type for the setup  menu. Formatting can be difficult and time consuming if you haven't done it before. For this reason, try to get the drive formatted before purchasing it.

&#9633; **Low noise**    Before purchasing a hard drive check to see how noisy it is, the quieter, obviously, the better.

Seagate has the largest share of the market for hard drives. While they offer many models of drives, a relatively inexpensive drive is the *Seagate ST 225*, it is however, not the most reliable. Its features include 20 Mb, 5 1/4 inch half height, a sluggish 65 ms, and stepper motor. Another and better drive is the *Micro Science HH 824*, 5 1/4 inch, half height, 61 ms, stepper motor. A reliable drive that can be used with an RLL controller is the *Miniscribe 3650,* 40 Mb (60 with an RLL controller), 61 ms, 5 1/4 inch, and half height. A newer 3 1/2 inch drive is the *Seagate ST 125*, 20 Mb, 36 ms, low noise and low power consumption.

# Expansion Tips

### Installing a New Hard Drive

XT clones do not come with the hard disk controller. It must be purchased as a separate card. The installation of a hard drive entails placing the hard disk controller card into an empty slot near the drive you wish to install. (Any slot will do, however). After this, it is a matter of installing the drive into an empty drive bay and attaching the cables to the proper connectors. The process for installing the drive is shown in Chapter 7. How to connect the ribbon cables is also shown.

It is important to have proper documentation on how to format the drive, or this process could be a nightmare. The drive can be formatted with either MS-DOS or with special hard disk formatting programs such as *SpeedStor* from **Storage Dimensions.** When using MS-DOS, the low level formatting or "physical format" is performed by running DEBUG, FDISK, and FORMAT. The procedure goes as follows, see the disk drive manual for complete instructions:

A>:DEBUG (enter)

- G = C800:5 (enter)

(answer questions)

A>: FDISK (enter)

(answer questions)

A>: FORMAT C:/s (enter)

(answer questions)

## Tips for Speeding Up the Hard Drive

Hard drives slow down as they fill up. This is especially true if the files are scattered or "fragmented" across the disk. This is because the drive has to search farther to locate data. One method to speed up the drive is to place the files one next to the other or "contiguously." In this case, the drive has to travel less distance to find the needed data. The result is that your application software will operate faster. Some software programs are designed to place files in this optimally contiguous fashion on the disk. One such disk optimizer programs is the **SoftLogic Systems** *Disk Optimizer*. (A Public Domain program to accomplish this can be ordered from the software section at the back of this book. The disk to order is the hard disk utility disk.)

Another way to speed up the operation of the hard drive is with disk-caching software. It offers a quick easy and inexpensive way to speed up the computer. This program sets aside a portion of RAM as a memory cache, where it stores the most often used data from the hard drive. When needed, the computer accesses this data quickly from the cache memory. This is much faster because data from RAM can be accessed as much as 10 times faster than it could be from the hard drive. A disk-caching program can speed up an actual application programs overall speed by as much as 300 percent. A couple of good disk caching programs are *Flash* by **Software Masters** and *Lightning* by the **Personal Computer Support Group**.

# Hard Disk Controllers

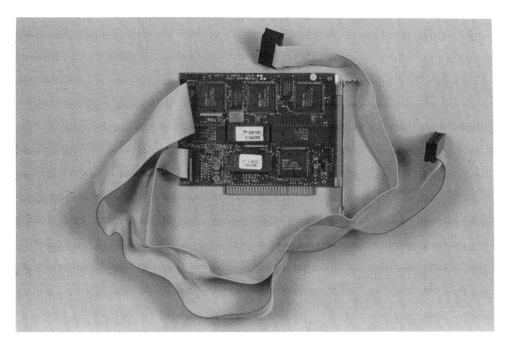

*Figure 6.40*    A hard disk controller

Every hard disk needs an interface card. The interface card for the hard disk is an 8-bit card called the hard disk controller. As computers gained higher performance, hard drives and controllers have, until recently, remained a bottleneck for speed and performance. For this reason, there is now a great deal of attention being paid to the development of higher performance hard disk controllers.

**MFM (Modified Frequency Modulation)**     MFM is a standard for encoding data onto the hard drive.  MFM controllers are the most common type available and have been around for the longest time.

**RLL Controllers (Run-Length Limited)**     Run-Length Limited is an improved encoding scheme devised by IBM.  An RLL controller compresses about 50% more data onto a hard drive.  A RLL-certified drive, however, is required in conjunction with this controller.

**SCSI (Small Computer Systems Interface)**     SCSI is a newer generation of controller.  It is compatible with the XT, AT, and 386 computers.  It has the advantage of higher performance and/or larger capacities.  Up to seven drives may be attached to a single SCSI controller allowing a total capacity as high as 2,000 megabytes.

## Buying Recommendations

Western Digital makes the majority of MFM controllers. **Western Digital** also makes some reliable RLL controllers. RLL controllers presently offer the best price/performance ratio. **Data Technology, Corp. (DTC)** offers the *5150* which contains a self configuring set up menu for easy formatting.  The *Sysgen SC 6000* has 16 K of static cache and supports a 1 to 1 interleave.

# Memory Expansion Cards

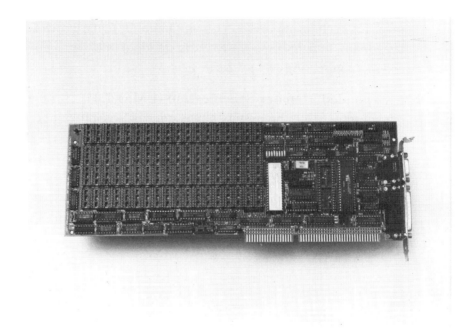

*Figure 6.41*    A 2 megabyte 16-bit memory card for an AT

The requirements for memory keep going up. Software application programs need more and more memory to operate efficiently. MS-DOS unfortunately only has the ability to access 640 K of memory directly. There are, however, some schemes which have been devised to indirectly get around the memory limits of DOS.

**Expanded Memory Specification (EMS)**    This was the first scheme to allow computers to use more memory.  It was written in 1985 by **Lotus, Intel**, and **Microsoft.**

**Enhanced Expanded Memory Specification (EEMS)** This competing and improved standard was created by some other large computer product manufacturers; namely, **AST**, **Quadram**, and **Ashton-Tate**.  This standard was better for multitasking applications than EMS.

**Expanded Memory Specification (EMS) 4.0**    All the companies supporting the previous two standards got together and merged the previous standards into yet another standard called EMS 4.0.  This is now the expanded memory standard on which everyone has agreed.  It allows for the use of up to 32 megabytes, the use of larger application software, and the use of multitasking.  It works on all generations of computers as well.

# Buying Recommendations

There are many different types of memory cards to choose from. Some cards can only be used as extended memory, others only as EMS, EMS 4.0, or EEMS while still others incorporate various combinations of the above.

**General tips**   The best boards to purchase use software to configure the board (this makes setup more convenient) and have diagnostic software which graphically shows where any defective chips are located  (thus making troubleshooting easier).

**0 K**   In advertisements you may see the term 0 K, this means that card comes with no, or "zero" memory. In this case. it will be up to you to add memory. Since the adding of memory chips can be relatively tedious, try to purchase the memory card "fully populated" with memory chips.

The type of card you should purchase depends on your application.

- ❑ If you need memory for a RAM drive, print spooler, or disk caching, then a board which offers plain extended memory is fine.

- ❑ If the software you want to operate only supports EMS, you may want to get this type of board. Bear in mind, that this type of memory management will soon be obsolete with EMS 4.0. Many switchable low cost Taiwanese EMS and extended memory boards are available.

- ❑ For multitasking an EMS 4.0 board would be desirable. With the use of special "drivers," many EEMS boards can be used with the EMS 4.0 standard.

## Expansion Tips

### Adding a Memory Card

A memory card is installed just as any other expansion card. For the physical installation into the computer see Chapter 7. Be sure the card comes with the proper configuration instructions. You may need to modify the CONFIG.SYS file.

## How to Create a RAM Drive

A RAM drive is made by allocating a portion of the computers RAM as an additional drive. The computer will automatically assigns this "virtual drive" the next available drive letter. The advantage of a RAM drive is that information can be quickly accessed (the information in the RAM drive is accessed up to 10 times faster than from a hard drive). However, if the computer is turned off, all information in the RAM drive will be lost.

MS-DOS has a program which allows you to create a RAM drive; it's called RAMDRIVE.SYS. In PC-DOS version 3.2 and above, it is called VDISK.SYS (for virtual disk). You can create a RAM drive by placing the appropriate commands in your CONFIG.SYS file. Following is an example of the line to place in the CONFIG.SYS for creating a 384 kilobyte RAM drive out of the computers 640K of memory.

```
DEVICE=RAMDRIVE.SYS 384 128 250
```

**384** is the amount of kilobytes of memory for the RAM disk. This figure is only limited by the amount of memory you have available.
**128** is the amount of bytes per sector.
**250** is the amount of files per directory.

If you are using PC-DOS, substitute RAMDRIVE.SYS with VDISK.SYS.

I just don't have enough memory to remember all this

# Modems

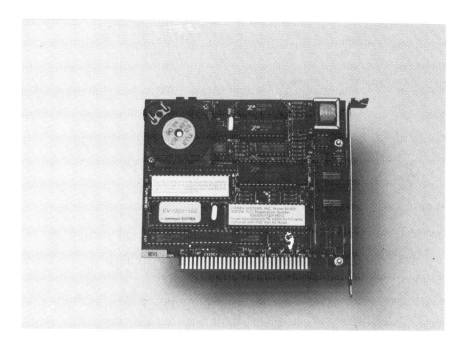

*Figure 6.42*    A 1200 baud modem

The modem (short for **mod**ulator/**dem**odulator) translates information from the computer into signals that can be sent over the telephone lines, and then another modem at the other end translates the signals back to something that the remote computer can understand.  Modems open up a whole world of possibilities; it is possible to transmit text and software all around the world. You can call local computer bulletin board services (BBS) and pick up public domain software or leave messages to fellow computer users.

I have set up a BBS for computer users to discuss different aspects of computing and for feedback on my books.  You are welcome to call and try out your modem. The number is (415) 522-9070. The parameters are as follows, 1200 baud, No parity, 8 data bits, 1 stop bit. The parameters govern the speed and manner of how data is transferred between modems. It is not so important to understand all the different parameters. Just remember that the parameters on your modem and those on the computer you are calling must match. Let's now look at some of the issues to be considered when purchasing a modem.

**Baud rate**    The baud rate is a measurement of the speed at which data can be transmitted. Some common speeds are 300, 1200, 2400, and 9600 baud.

**Internal versus external**    The internal modem is an expansion card which plugs into a slot in the computer. An external modem has its own housing and sits next to the computer; it connects with a cable to the computer's serial port. The external modem takes its power from an outlet via a transformer.

**Hayes compatible**    A de facto standard for the way software controls the operation of the modem was created by **Hayes Micro Computer Products, Inc**. The overwhelming majority of 300, 1200,  and 2400 baud modem manufacturers follow this standard. Therefore, when purchasing a modem be sure it is **Hayes** compatible. Unfortunately, there is  no clear standard for modems above 2400 baud.

## Buying Recommendations

For most users, an internal modem is best. It keeps the desk uncluttered and is less expensive because it doesn't require a housing, transformer, serial port, and cable. The advantages of the external modem are that it contains LED status lights which indicate important handshaking signals, carrier signals, etc., and it does not require an expansion slot. Also, it is easily disconnected and attached onto any computer or terminal as long as the computer or terminal has a serial port.

*Figure 6.43*    "I'd really rather be using a modem"

The price of modems has fallen dramatically over the last year or so. An internal 1200 baud modem can be purchased for as low as $75 and a 2400 baud modem for about double that.

If you are transferring lots of data, or have money to spare, get a 2400 baud modem. If you don't use the modem very often, a 1200 baud modem should be fine. Until a standard emerges for the 4800 baud and above modems, I would avoid these unless you are transferring massive amounts of data. Some good inexpensive modems are made by **Practical Peripherals**, **Everex**, and **Smarteam**.

# Expansion Tips

### Adding a Modem

The process of adding an internal modem is very easy. The physical installation only involves opening the computer and inserting the modem into an empty expansion slot. Use the instructions in Chapter 7 for the actual installation. The area that might cause problems are the COM settings. You must make sure that the modem does not conflict with other serial ports. Double check the modem documentation for the proper COM setting.

### Telecommunications software

Every modem requires a communications program to operate. An excellent public domain telecommunications program I have found is **ProComm**; it has a feature that allows you to automate dialing: with one key stroke it calls the number, enters your name, enters your password, etc. on the remote computer. This program is available by sending in the software coupon in the back of this book.

*Carbon Copy* by **Meridian Technology** is a commercial program which allows you to call another computer and gives you the ability to control, transfer files, monitor and use software running on a remote PC. Using this program, a colleague in Texas and I in San Francisco were able to simultaneously work on the manuscript of this book in a word processing program.

A telecommunications service I have found quite useful has been *PC Pursuit* from **GTE Sprint**. For a flat fee of only $25 per month, you can make an unlimited number of data connections to 25 cities on weeknights (from 6 pm to 7 am) and all day on weekends and holidays. The number to call for more information and registration is 1-800-TELENET.

# Ports

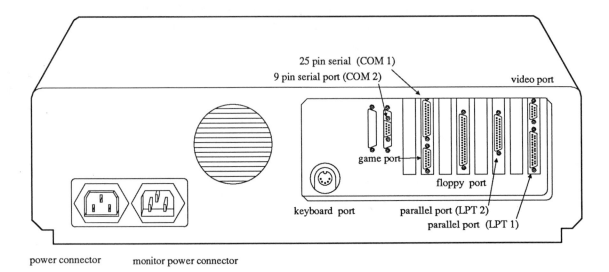

*Figure 6.44*     The back of the computer showing the various ports

Ports are connectors in the back of the computer which send and receive date to and from the peripherals. The types of ports used in an XT include serial, parallel, video, game, floppy drive and keyboard ports. They are used to connect peripherals such as modems, monitors, printers, plotters, and keyboards. Ports can be found directly on the motherboard but most are added with the use of separate expansion cards which fit into expansion slots.

Let's take a closer look at some of these ports.

**Serial Ports**    These are 25 pin male connectors which are used to connect the computer to a mouse, external modem, serial printer, plotter, graphic tablet or even another computer. There are two types, 9 pin and 25 pin. The 9 pin is more frequently used on 286 and 386 computers but is sometimes used on the XTs. The serial port itself is also referred to as an RS232. RS232 is a standard for serial communications, used in virtually all microcomputers.

Serial ports are called serial because they send and receive information *serially*, or in other words, one bit at a time. These ports are also referred to as **COM** ports. The XT will typically have

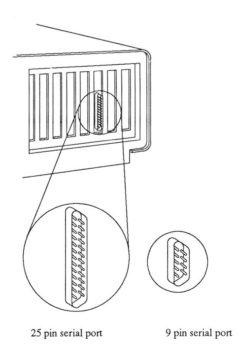

25 pin serial port          9 pin serial port

*Figure 6.45*     A 25 pin and 9 pin serial port

two COM ports.  Each COM port is defined as either COM1 or COM2.

**The null modem cable**    The serial port connects to different devices with a cable.  For some devices, or for the connecting of two computers together via the serial port, a special cable is needed.  It is referred to as a null modem cable.  This cable reverses pins 2 and 3, the transmit and receive pins so that the serial port can both send and receive data.

*Figure 6.46*    Two types of port

**Parallel Ports**   Parallel ports are 25 pin female connectors. They send data in parallel, that is, 8 bits at a time. These ports are designated as **LPT** ports. LPT is an abbreviation for *line printer*, a device commonly used with this port. Just as COM ports have a number, so do parallel ports. XTs typically have two parallel ports which are always defined as LPT1 or LPT2.

**Game Port**   This 15 pin female connector is used for joysticks and paddles. These are usually used to interface with game software.

**Keyboard**   This 5 pin female connector connects the keyboard or a bar code reader to the computer.

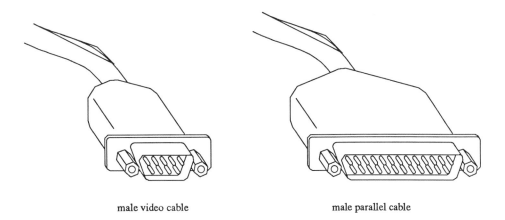

male video cable                    male parallel cable

*Figure 6.47*   The connectors on the video and parallel cables

**Video Port**    This 9 pin female port connects to a monochrome, CGA or EGA monitor.  VGA monitors, however, connect to a 15 pin female connector.

**Power Connector**    This 3 pin male plug is located on the power supply and connects to the electrical power cable.

**Floppy Drive Port**    Many floppy disk controllers can support up to four floppy disk drives.  Two are usually connected inside the computer.  The 37 pin female connector found on the back of the card is for the connection of a ribbon cable, that attaches in a chain fashion, to the third and fourth drive.

**Monitor Power Connector**    This 3 prong female connector is found on the power supply next to the power connector.  The power supply in IBM computers was designed so that a monitor could be connected to the computer's power supply.  This was done so that the computer and monitor could be turned on with just one switch.  This became common for most power supply manufacturers.  Most monitors however, do not have the special male connector and come with the standard wall outlet plug.

# CHAPTER 7

# HOW TO ASSEMBLE AN XT CLONE

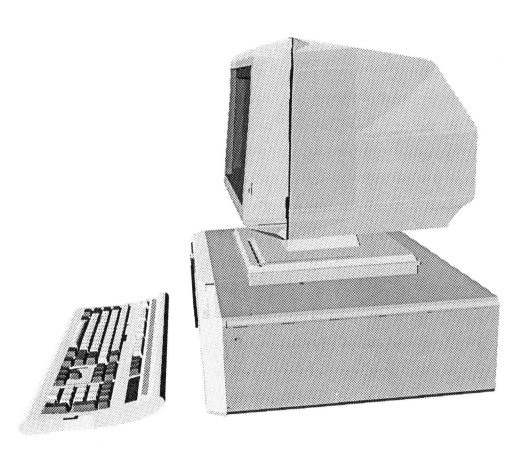

## Chapter Focus

This chapter takes you through the steps for assembling an XT clone. The text is supported with appropriate illustrations which further makes this task a cinch for even the novice.

*Figure 7.1*   Anyone can assemble a computer

\* \* \* \* \*

ANYONE CAN assemble a computer if one chooses to do
so.  It is not a very difficult task since it only entails putting
together eight or ten parts.  There is no soldering and the only
tools required for the process are a screw driver and possibly a
socket with driver.  All the parts snap together and the assembly
process can generally be done in two hours.

   There are however, several possible drawbacks to putting
together your own computer.  First, as has previously been stated
in this book, you don't save much (if any) money doing the computer assembly yourself.  The price that the seller adds for
assembling the machine is usually negligible, often only $25 or
less.  The time it would take you to do the work could perhaps be
used more productively elsewhere.  In assembling the parts yourself, you also run a minor risk of damaging the machine.  The

seller usually is very adept at this task since it is a normal part of his selling procedure to do the assembling. (And if he or she damages it, you don't have to pay for it).

On the other hand, there are certain advantages to be gained from assembling your computer yourself. You will learn more about how the computer hardware works and this will make the computer more approachable for future hardware-oriented tasks which may arise. You will feel more confident about such tasks as replacing individual components, should they malfunction. Installing upgrades and enhancements would also be a more approachable task. Aside from all this confidence building, do-it-yourself expansion and upgrade installations can save you considerable money since technicians sometimes can charge up to $70 per hour for their time.

*Figure 7.2*    You will gain confidence from the assembly experience

# Important! Before You Begin!

Read this guide carefully before you begin shopping for parts. Be sure to purchase all the parts from **one** dealer. You will then have only one dealer to return to in the event you run into problems. Also, when buying, make sure you get the proper documentation with the hardware you purchase. You can waste a great deal of time by not having adequate documentation and information. Check the documentation to see that it shows pin connectors, jumper configurations, and dip switch settings. Also, be sure it's written in good English.

### Flip-Top versus *AT Style* Chassis

It should also be kept in mind that there are different cases, screws, drives, etc. available...each with slight variations in hardware, shape, size, locations of mounting points, and so forth. Keep in mind that your specific hardware may be a little different. This chapter will show how to assemble the standard XT flip-top chassis and one of the newer *AT style chassis. The instructions which pertain only to the AT style chassis are in italics.*

### About Static Electricity

One important preliminary precaution should be stated at this point. Static electricity can damage computer chips. Generally, static electricity is not a big problem. However, it is a good idea to ground yourself by touching the metal chassis of your computer, before touching any chips. This will discharge any static electricity stored in your body.

## Typical Tools List

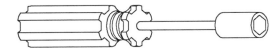

❏   One socket and driver set

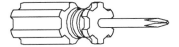

❏   One medium size Phillips screw driver

*Figure 7.3*   Fortunately, building an XT clone only requires a few tools

## Typical Parts List

❑ Flip top or AT style chassis and hardware accessories consisting of:

  [1]  Drive bay covers

  [2]  Drive plate

  [3]  Plastic guides (for holding expansion cards)

  [4]  Brass standoffs (for mounting the motherboard)

  [5]  Expansion card slot covers

  [6]  (4) rubber feet pads (for bottom of chassis)

  [7]  Speaker and holder

  [8]  A variety of screws

  [9]  *Nylon standoffs*

❑ Power supply

❑ Floppy disk drive(s)

❑ Keyboard

❑ Motherboard

❑ Floppy disk controller card with (1) ribbon cable

❑ Display card

❑ Monitor

❑ Optional accessories: modem, hard disk and controller, memory expansion card, multi I/O card etc.

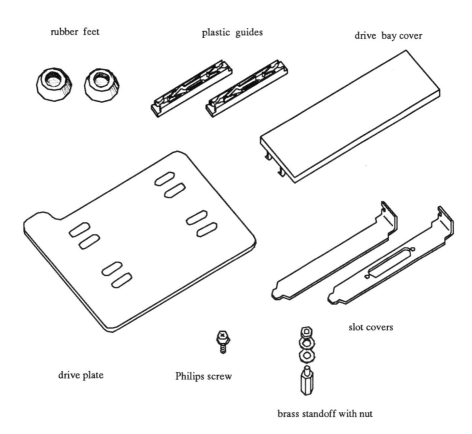

rubber feet                    plastic guides                    drive bay cover

drive plate              Philips screw                    slot covers

brass standoff with nut

*Figure 7.4*    Hardware for XT chassis

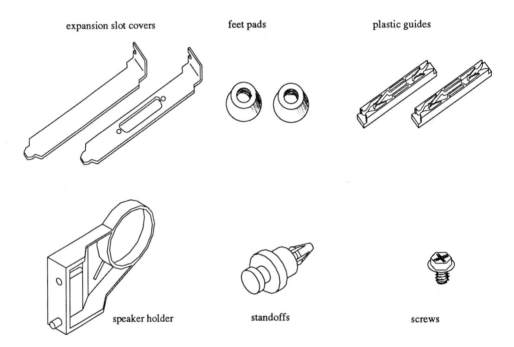

expansion slot covers          feet pads               plastic guides

speaker holder                standoffs                 screws

*Figure 7.5    Hardware for AT style chassis*

# Assembly Instructions

## [A] Checking the Parts

[1] Open all the packages of parts and make sure that everything looks okay. The solder on the boards should look cleanly flowed and there should be no obvious broken wires, etc. Open the package containing the screws. Arrange each of the same-sized parts and screws into their own piles.

## [B] Preparing the Chassis

[1] Attach the plastic card guides to the back of the card guide panel with appropriate screws. (These plastic guides are used to support full length expansion cards).

[2] Glue or place the speaker over the speaker opening, usually located under the drive rack on the bottom of the chassis.

[3] *With the AT style chassis if it has not already been preassembled, place the speaker in the speaker holder. Attach the holder in the space behind the front panel with a single screw to the top of the card guide panel.*

**4**   *If the LED/keylock assembly has not been installed, screw it to the front panel of the computer. The green LED is for "power on" while the red LED is for "hard drive accessing" and the yellow one is for "turbo on."*

**5**   Place the 4 rubber feet on the underside of the chassis. It may be necessary to use a spot of glue to make sure they stick properly.

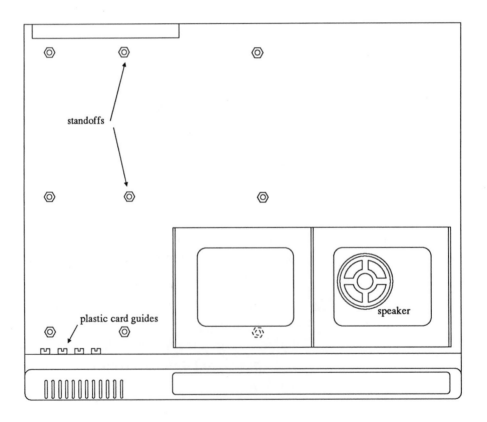

*Figure 7.6*  The chassis

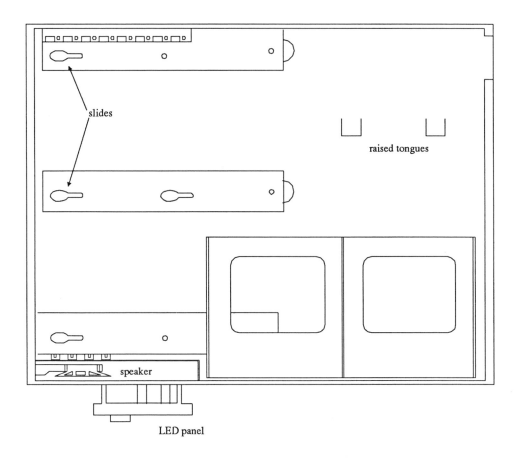

*Figure 7.7    The AT style chassis*

## [C]  Preparing the Motherboard

[1]  Be sure to get adequate documentation with the motherboard. There are a wide variety of different ways to prepare the motherboard, install the memory and BIOS (Basic Input/Output System) chips, set the jumpers and dip switches, and connect the various wires. Check your documentation for the proper settings.

[2]  Insert the memory chips with the half-moon orientation notches or other markings facing the same way as other previously installed chips. In other words, the memory chips should all be facing the same way on the motherboard. Set the DIP switches according to the manufacturers instructions (usually switches three and four are for memory). The DIP switches are necessary to recognize the amount of memory installed (see motherboard documentation or page 284).

[3]  If the BIOS chip has not yet been installed, install it now. Refer to the owner's manual of the motherboard for the proper placement of the BIOS.

[4]  Check all pins on the chips to make sure they are firmly seated into their sockets and no pins are bent or folded under the chips.

[5]  *See where the holes on the motherboard match the slides on the chassis. Then place the standoffs into the holes that match the slide positions on the motherboard.*

# Typical DIP Switch Settings

SW 1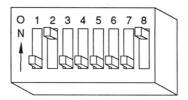

## Normal Operation Switch #1

| | |
|---|---|
| **1 OFF** | normal operation |

## Coprocessor Switch #2

| | |
|---|---|
| **2 ON** | board has no 8087 co-processor |
| **2 OFF** | board has 8087 co-processor |

## Memory Switches #3 and #4

| | | |
|---|---|---|
| **3 OFF** | **4 ON** | 128K memory installed |
| **3 ON** | **4 OFF** | 192K memory installed |
| **3 OFF** | **4 OFF** | 256K memory or more installed |

## Display Adaptor Switches #5 and #6

| | | |
|---|---|---|
| **5 ON** | **6 ON** | No Display Adaptor, EGA, or VGA |
| **5 OFF** | **6 ON** | Color Graphics Adaptor (40 x 20 mode) |
| **5 ON** | **6 OFF** | Color Graphics Adaptor (80 x 20 mode) |
| **5 OFF** | **6 OFF** | Monochrome Display Adaptor or both.) |

## Disk Drives Switches #7 and #8

| | | |
|---|---|---|
| **7 ON** | **8 ON** | one drive installed |
| **7 OFF** | **8 ON** | two drives installed |
| **7 ON** | **8 OFF** | three drives installed |
| **7 OFF** | **8 OFF** | four drives are installed |

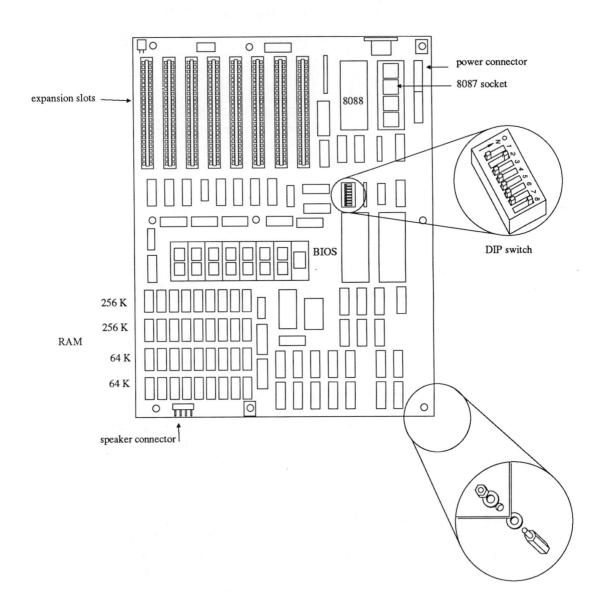

*Figure 7.8*    XT clone motherboard

*Figure 7.9*    An actual XT clone motherboard

## D   Installing the Motherboard

1   Use the proper screws and from the bottom of the chassis, attach the remaining eight brass standoffs to the chassis with their threads facing up. Leave the standoffs somewhat loose now so you'll have some play in them to line them up with the holes in the motherboard.

2   Place a fiber insulating washer on each brass standoff.

3   Orient the motherboard with the 8 expansion slots facing the rear. Slide the motherboard into place over the standoffs.

4   Line up the standoff threads with the holes. This may take a little gentle jiggling of the motherboard.

5   Place an insulating washer on each brass standoff and tighten with the proper nuts. You may have to use a screwdriver to keep the screws on the bottom of the chassis from turning.

6   *Present the motherboard so that the plastic standoffs are facing the slides in the chassis floor, making sure that all nylon standoffs are inside the holes. Then push the board sideways till it is firmly in place.*

7   *Two to four screws are used to fasten and ground the motherboard to the chassis. Care should be taken not to deform or warp the motherboard. The screws should be snug, not overly tight.*

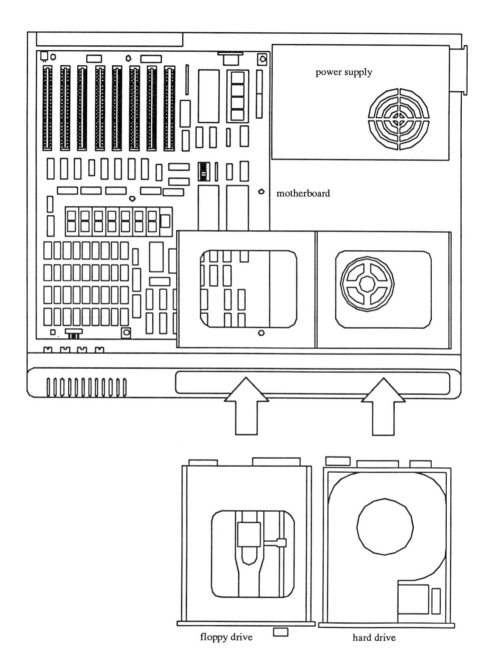

*Figure 7.10*    Internal layout

8  *Check the motherboard documentation for the proper connections and then connect the green power-on LED, turbo switch, turbo LED, reset switch, and keylock switch to the proper pins. The lock disables the keyboard so that others cannot disturb your program when you are away from the computer. In some chassis, it also locks the case so that no one can open the computer and steal the expansion cards. (They can, of course, still walk off with the whole computer).*

9  Plug the speaker into the pin connector on the motherboard. Connect any other wires to their respective pins. (See motherboard documentation).

## E⟩ Installing the Power Supply

1⟩ Place the power supply on the bottom of the chassis and slide it, so that, the raised tongues catch on the cutouts on the bottom of the power supply.

2⟩ Slide the power supply toward the back of the chassis and secure it with four screws from the rear of the chassis.

3⟩ Connect the power cable(s) to pins on the motherboard. The correct pins are the ones nearest the power supply. Normally the power cable only connects one way. The three red wires should be toward the front of the computer.

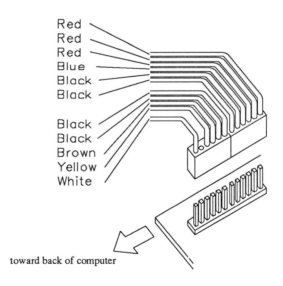

*Figure 7.11*    Connecting the power supply to the motherboard

## F  Installing the Floppy Drives

1   Make sure the jumpers on the drives are set properly
    and remove terminating resistors as necessary . This
    can be a confusing step if you don't have the instruc-
    tions for the proper jumper settings.  Each drive
    model can have a different setting.

2   Note: it may be easier (depending on the chassis) to
    connect the power cables and the controller cables
    before securing drives.  Connect power cables from
    the power supply to the drives; they connect only
    one way.  Be sure they are firmly seated.

3   In the flip-top chassis, the drives can be arranged in
    the drive bays as you wish; both on the left side
    (facing the front of the computer), both on the right
    side, or both across the bottom.  It's easiest to place
    them both on the left side.  Just slide the drives in
    from the front and secure them with the proper
    screws.  The metal plate is used to secure the other
    side of the drives.  Secure the bottom of the drives
    through the holes in the bottom of the chassis.  A
    trick to use; put some glue on the tip of your screw
    driver during this step.  Otherwise it's hard to get
    the screws into place without dropping them.

4   *The floppy drives go on the right side (when you are
    facing the front) of the chassis.  The A: drive is
    typically placed in the top drive bay.  B: drive goes
    on the bottom. Just slide the drives in from the front.
    Secure the drives with two screws to the side and
    two from the bottom of the chassis.  A trick to use;*

*put some glue or rubber cement on the tip of your screw driver during this step. Otherwise it's hard to get the screws into place without dropping them. The metal plate is used to secure the other side of the drives.*

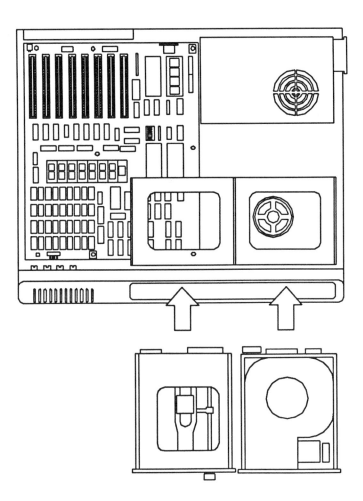

*Figure 7.12*    Ínstalling drive in the flip-top chassis

## G  Installing the Floppy Controller

1  Expansion cards can be plugged into any of the expansion slots on the motherboard; the computer will detect what and where they are.

2  Insert the floppy drive controller or Multi I/O into a slot near the drives. To get it to go into the slot, use a firm back-and-forth rocking motion.

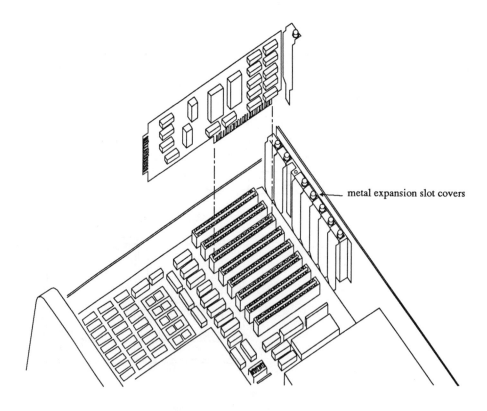

metal expansion slot covers

*Figure 7.13*    Installing expansion cards

## H  Connecting the Cables to Floppy Drives

1  Using the supplied cable, connect the controller card to the floppy drives. The colored line on all the ribbon cables always connect to the number-one pin on the controller and toward the notch on the drive side.

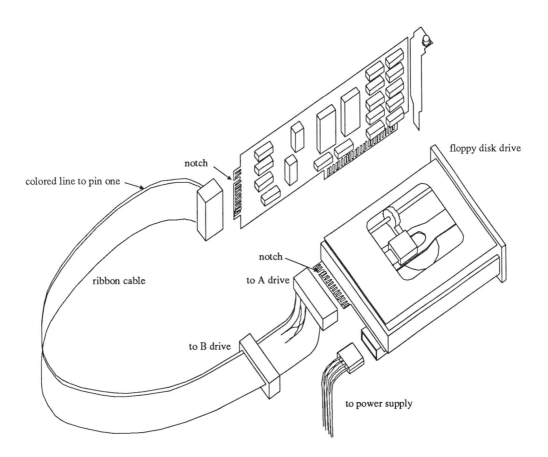

*Figure 7.14*    Connecting the controller to the floppy drive

## Ⅰ   Installing the Hard Disk

**1**   Slide the hard drive into the left drive bay and secure it with the 2 screws from the side and two from the bottom of the chassis. Again, put some glue on the tip of your screw driver during this step. Otherwise it's hard to get the screws into place without dropping them.

**2**   Connect the power cable from the power supply to the hard drive. Again it connects only one way.

## Ⅰ   Installing the Hard Disk Controller

**1**   Insert the hard disk controller into a slot near the drives. To get it to go into the slot, use a firm back-and-forth rocking motion.

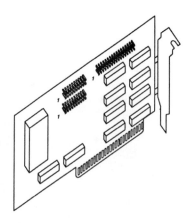

*Figure 7.15*    The hard disk controller

## K   Connecting the Cables to the Hard Drive

1   Connect the thin data cable from the controller to the hard-disk drive. Connect the larger cable in the same manner. The colored line on the cable goes to the number-one pin on the controller and toward the notch on the hard drive side.

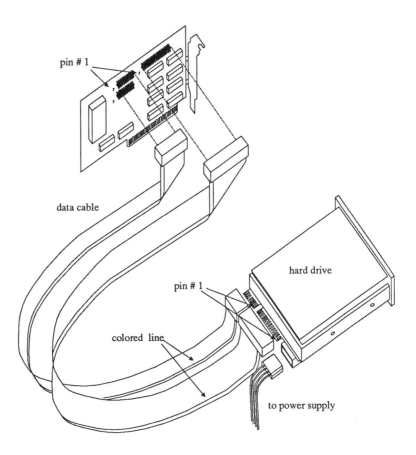

*Figure 7.16*    Connecting cables to the hard drive

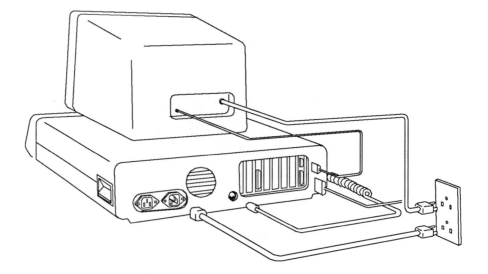

*Figure 7.17*    External connections

## ⬛L⬛ Installing the Monitor Display Card

⬛1⬛ Plug the display card into the motherboard. It can go into any slot. It is usually placed into the slot farthest from the power supply.

## ⬛M⬛ Finishing Up

⬛1⬛ Install any other cards such as expanded memory cards, modem, etc. Make sure all cards are firmly seated in the expansion slots. Screw them down to the chassis.

⬛2⬛ Screw the card slot covers to the back of the chassis. Fasten all expansion cards down as well.

⬛3⬛ Close the lid or *slide the cover from the front to the back of the computer.* Secure the cover with five screws to the rear of the chassis.

## ⬛N⬛ External Connections

⬛1⬛ Plug the monitor power cable to a wall outlet and the connector to the back of the display card.

⬛2⬛ Connect the keyboard to the keyboard connector in the back of the computer.

⬛3⬛ Connect the power cable from the power supply to the wall outlet.

## ⬚ Testing and Configuring Your Computer

⬚ If the computer doesn't work properly right away, go back and check over your work. First check to see if you have performed all the steps. Second, check to see if all assembly steps were done correctly. Especially make sure the memory chips and BIOS were inserted correctly and that no pins on the chips are bent. Next, double check all the connection and the DIP switch settings. If the computer still does not function correctly, check Chapter Eight, the Troubleshooting Chapter for further possible resolutions to the problem.

## Congratulations!

You have now successfully assembled your own computer and are the proud owner of an XT clone. Happy computing!

# CHAPTER 8

# TROUBLESHOOTING YOUR COMPUTER

# Chapter Focus

A "bug" can turn up in any computer. This chapter prepares you for, and leads you through, the process of "debugging" or troubleshooting a computer. A unique method of using a hardware flow chart to systematically track down computer malfunctions and anomalies is outlined in the last part of the chapter.

*Figure 8.1*    There are many different ways to troubleshoot a computer

※ ※ ※ ※ ※

ANYONE CAN troubleshoot a computer. It is not as difficult as you might think. In fact, there are only eight or ten individual parts to deal with in troubleshooting the typical computer. You don't need any elaborate testing equipment; a regular flat blade screw driver, a needle nose plier, and a Phillips screw driver are generally enough to deal with most problems.

Because of the computer's modular design, repairs are performed by exchanging a defective part with a properly functioning one. There is no soldering of wires or anything messy, difficult, or tedious with the exchanging of parts. While it is possible to do repair work on a faulty part, a straight exchange is much easier and usually the most cost-effective route to take. The reason for this is that most parts cost below $150, and with labor costs being what they are, it is generally more expensive to have the part repaired. The only parts that are worth having repaired are those which cost over $150.

# Who Should Do the Troubleshooting?

The very first decision that you will need to make when you have trouble with your computer is to determine who will do the servicing or troubleshooting. The following are some of the options:

☐ If the computer is still under warranty, take it back to the dealer from whom you purchased the computer. It is the dealer's responsibility to honor the warranty and resolve any problems. If the computer is beyond the warranty period, you can still take the computer to the dealer from whom you initially purchased it. The dealer is likely to be the most qualified person to work on it, since he assembles and troubleshoots them on a regular basis. He will use the same techniques that are outlined later in this chapter. There may, in fact, be certain advantages for the consumer in having a dealer do the troubleshooting. These possible advantages include the following:

   ☛ The dealer will likely have the most knowledge and experience about what the possible failures or problems could be.

   ☛ He also has the advantage of having readily available replacement parts and may be able to repair it faster than you (or someone else) could.

   ☛ He may be inclined (since you bought the computer from him in the first place) to charge you less for the repairs than perhaps some other dealer. The labor charges for troubleshooting are typically from $50 to $60 an hour, plus the cost of any parts which need replacing.

❏   Another option is to take the computer to a
    different dealer (other than the one you purchased
    the computer from).  Most dealers will be able to
    perform repairs.  Computer dealers (both clone
    dealers and otherwise) are listed in the Yellow
    Pages under "Computer Dealers."  Labor costs
    will be (as previously stated) between $50 to $60
    per hour, plus the cost of any replacement parts.)

❏   Yet another possibility is that you can call in a
    computer repair person who comes to your home
    or office and does the repairs "on-site."  This
    approach is hassle free since you don't have to
    carry the computer all over town, however, it can
    be expensive.  On-site service technicians can be
    found in the Yellow Pages under "Computer Ser-
    vicing and Repair" or through word of mouth.
    (Labor costs are typically $55 to $75 per hour,

*Figure 8.2*     Sometimes it's best to call in a specialist to do the job

plus parts costs. An extra "on site" service charge may also be applied.)

❏ Another possibility is that you can take the computer to a specialized computer repair shop. Such repair shops can also be found in the Yellow Pages; look under "Computer Servicing and Repair." (The fee ranges from $50 to $70 per hour plus the cost of replacing parts).

❏ Yet another possibility is that you can have a friend who is familiar with computers repair it. He or she might do it for free to help you out (this can be a great excuse to take your friend to dinner), or do some kind of trade.

❏ Still another approach to troubleshooting is the user group. User groups are usually full of people who are knowledgeable regarding computer hardware. At a user group meeting you can talk to fellow members about your computer troubles. The member of such groups often swap troubleshooting stories and tips. The group might actually help you do the troubleshooting.

❏ The final option to consider is doing the repair yourself. As mentioned earlier, anyone can perform computer repairs. As with everything else in life, there are also pros and cons to troubleshooting your own computer. These include:

### Pros

☞ You will save money if you do the troubleshooting yourself. Replacement parts will be your only cost.

☞ You may save "down time" by quickly fixing a problem yourself. In other words, you don't have to wait for some overworked repair technician, who may take a few weeks before he has time to work on your system.

☞ You will continue to gain confidence and learn about your computer. The repair process can be fun, and you can gain a great deal of satisfaction from having done it yourself. It will help you become familiar with your computer and this knowledge will be useful for doing any kind of computer expansion later on.

## Cons

☞ You may not have time, and it may be a hassle.

☞ A dealer may be able to do the job much faster.

☞ You may need spare parts for the actual troubleshooting process – and these parts may not be available. (The instructions in this chapter depend heavily on the ability of having spare parts to swap out with possible defective parts.) The temporary replacement of a part is the easiest way, and in many cases, the only way to conclusively narrow down a problem. In all likelihood, as an owner of a single computer, you may not have these spare parts around. You may need to find some parts for the troubleshooting process. This situation can be resolved by borrowing parts from a friend or a fellow user group member who has a similar computer. Or, if you are in an office with other computers around, you can momentarily borrow parts from these computers.

# Doing the Troubleshooting Yourself

## Learning How to do Troubleshooting

Before actually doing any computer troubleshooting, you may want to learn a bit more about how to do it. There are several possible ways to do this. They include the following points:

- ❑ **Read books on troubleshooting** There are several books available, however, the ones I've seen go into too much detail. They explain such sophisticated matters as how to take apart drives and how to do soldering on a circuit board. This is much too complicated and time consuming for the average user.

- ❑ **Talk to friends** See what your friends have done in the way of troubleshooting. What problems did they experience with their equipment and how did they deal with them.

- ❑ **Join a user group** Members of user groups often exchange information on how to deal with difficulties. Some user groups have question-and-answer periods that would be an opportune moment to bring up any unresolved questions you may have. The feedback you get could be invaluable.

- ❑ **Learn by doing** The more troubleshooting you do, the more knowledge you will acquire, and the easier any future repairs (or expansions) will be.

- ❑ **And of course,** study the instructions in this chapter.

## General Pointers

- **Relax**    If while troubleshooting, you are going crazy trying to find the problem, do something else for a while.  Leave it for the next day and get a good rest.  It's amazing how often, after sleeping on the problem, an answer may just pop into your head.

- **Work systematically**    The computer parts are connected together in a systematic and logical order.  When you are troubleshooting, be sure to work systematically and check each part that could possibly be causing the problem.

*Figure 8.3*    The PC Clone User Group troubleshooting team

# The Three Basic Sources of Problems

The three basic causes of computer problems are human error, software malfunction, and hardware malfunction. When working systematically, you will first want to eliminate the first two type of errors as the possible source of the problem.

## Human Error

Frequently, the cause of a problem is human error. The user may have done something incorrect which causes the computer to work incorrectly. Some common human errors are:

- ❏ Lack of familiarity with the software.
- ❏ An incorrect command being executed in the software.
- ❏ A wrong key being punched.
- ❏ The hardware not being plugged in and turned on.
- ❏ Not placing the disk in the correct drive.
- ❏ Forgetting to close the drive door.

## Software Malfunction

Each piece of software has its own "personality" and can have bugs or problems which have nothing to do with the hardware. Problems which show up on your screen after the A:> prompt are usually software-related. Since this book is primarily hardware-oriented, it is not appropriate that this chapter mention all the possible software-related problems. If you have problems with the software, a good starting place is to consult the manual of that particular piece of software for possible remedies.

Another possibility is to call the software manufacturer's technical support line. Also check your AUTOEXEC.BAT and CONFIG.SYS files. Often erratic computer problems are caused by conflicting programs and commands in these two files. The solution is to remove some or all of the commands and see if the computer still has a problem.

## Hardware Malfunction

Problems which show up on your screen before the A:> prompt are usually hardware-related. The following sections in this chapter show how to deal systematically with hardware-related problems.

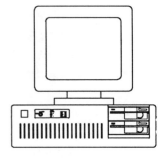

# The Techniques for Diagnosing Hardware Problems

There are two methods of finding a hardware-related problem. The first method is "diagnosing with troubleshooting software." This entails the use of special software programs which examine the hardware and attempts to find the problem. This method, of course, requires that the computer be in an operational state. The second method is "diagnosing with a Hardware Flow Chart." This method consists of systematically using a flow chart to track down the cause of a problem.

## Diagnosing with Troubleshooting Software

### Built-in Computer Self Test

There is an error-detection routine imbedded in the BIOS; it is called the Power-On Self Test (POST). Every time the computer is turned on, it does a general self test on the main components of the computer. This test gives audio error beeps, numeric error codes, and plain English error messages that refer to specific parts of the computer. These messages can vary from computer brand to computer brand; however, they tend to follow the original IBM set of error messages. The following error messages discussed here are those used by IBM and most clone manufacturers.

# Typical Audio Error Codes

| Error Beep | Problem |
|---|---|
| A short beep | Everything is normal |
| A long continuous beep | A key on the keyboard may be stuck |
| Nothing, a continuous beep, or a series of short beeps | Power supply |
| One long beep and one short beep | Motherboard |
| One long beep and 2 short beeps | Monitor or cable problem |
| Normal short beep with the drive light staying on | Drive and/or drive controller |

**The Numeric Error Code**    If the computer finds a problem with one of the parts during its self-test, it gives a numeric or English error message.  The table on the following page shows a table with a partial listing of what the numeric codes refer to. For a more complete list, see Appendix D.

**The "Memory Parity Check"**    Another part of the Power-On Self Test is a memory check.  The computer runs through each RAM chip to test for possible malfunctions.  If an anomaly is detected, an error message pops up on the screen saying "Parity Error" with some numbers behind it.  Unfortunately these numbers are difficult to decipher because they vary from computer to computer.

# Numeric Error Codes

| Error number | Problem |
|---|---|
| 100-199 | Motherboard |
| 200-299 | Memory |
| 300-399 | Keyboard |
| 400-499 | Monochrome monitor |
| 500-599 | Color monitor |
| 600-699 | Floppy drive |
| 700-799 | Math coprocessor |
| 900-999 | Parallel printer port |
| 1100-1199 | Serial port |
| 1300-1399 | Game port |
| 1400-1499 | Printer |
| 1700-1799 | Hard drive |
| 2400-2499 | EGA |

## IBM Diagnostic Software

You can use the diagnostic software that comes with either the IBM XT (or the close compatibles) "Manual Of Operations." For XT clone owners, this software may not be readily available.

## Public Domain Diagnostic Software

Many diagnostic software programs have been written by individuals and are available through public domain software channels. I have compiled a series of tests into one diskette and it is available by sending in the software coupon in the back of this book. These very helpful programs do such functions as measure the speed of the computer, check the speed of the hard drive, check the RAM for errors, check the ports to make sure they're functioning properly and give a list of all the parts which are in the computer (such as display card type, types of ports, number of drives installed, etc).

### Advanced Diagnostic Software

Advanced diagnostic software programs are available from various companies. Two such helpful programs are *QAPlus* from **DiagSoft, Inc.** and the *Landmark Diagnostic Utility* from **Landmark Software.** There are other highly technical diagnostic software packages but they are expensive and difficult for the average person to come by. They are more suitable for the serious technician. They contain lots of complicated documentation and tend to be too technical or time-consuming to learn for doing casual repairs.

# Diagnosing with a Hardware Flow chart

The flow chart on the following page shows how all the parts interconnect including the path of probable cause of a problem. If you have problems with one of these parts, systematically follow the logical sequence of how the part connects to each other part – while making sure each part is functioning properly.

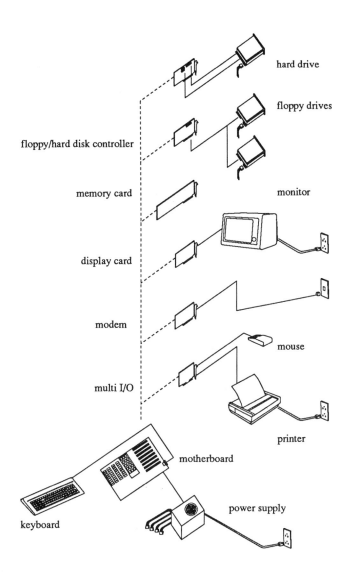

hard drive

floppy drives

floppy/hard disk controller

memory card

monitor

display card

modem

multi I/O

mouse

printer

motherboard

keyboard

power supply

*Figure 8.4*    Computer system troubleshooting flow chart

# Symptoms and Possible Cures

This section lists different symptoms which you may encounter with each part. After each symptom, there are a series of points to check in an effort to track down and isolate the problem.

**WARNING!!!!** Don't work on the insides of the computer with the power on. Turn off the computer and disconnect the power cord before opening the computer.

## Troubleshooting the System Unit

(The "system unit" is the basic computer box, i.e. chassis, motherboard, and power supply.)

⟨!⟩ **Computer does not turn on and appears completely dead.**

- ❑ Is the power switch turned on?
- ❑ Is there power from the wall outlet? Plug a lamp into the wall socket to make sure power is available.
- ❑ Is the power cord properly connected to the wall outlet and the computer power socket? Does the cord look OK and undamaged? If it looks damaged, replace it.
- ❑ Open the system unit and push down on all chips to make sure they are seated properly.
- ❑ Check the power connector from the power supply to the motherboard.
- ❑ Check for loose wire or foreign object such as a screw on nut causing a short.

❏ Jiggle all the connections inside and outside of the computer

❏ Pull out and reinsert all the cards; try placing them in different slots. (The connections may be corroded).

❏ Take out all non-essential parts (such as modem, multi I/O cards, memory cards, and hard drive) so that only the basic parts such as the motherboard, power supply, display card, controller and drive are left. Does the computer work now? If so, replace each part, one at a time, until the problem reoccurs. When you replace a part and the computer stops working, you know that part is the reason for the problem. It can then be replaced.

❏ If the computer still doesn't operate, remove all the remaining cards including the display card and floppy controller – turn on the power and check if the power supply fan is running. If it runs, one of the cards you just removed is bad.

❏ If the computer doesn't work with the minimal parts installed, start replacing each of the remaining parts, beginning with the power supply. (Be sure to turn the power off before reinserting a card). First swap out the power supply; next, the display card, then the drive controller, and finally the motherboard.

⟨!⟩ **There is a smell of smoke.**

❏ Shut off the computer.

❏ Open up the computer to determine the reason. It is usually a capacitor or battery that has burned out (or in the case of one XT I saw, exploded from heat). The faulty component will most likely be blackened or ash gray. Replace the damaged subassembly.

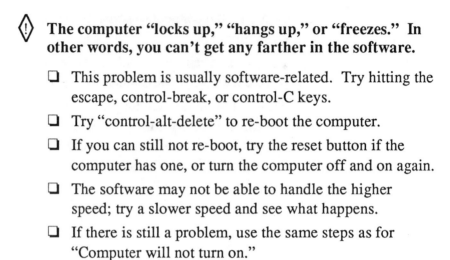

**The computer "locks up," "hangs up," or "freezes." In other words, you can't get any farther in the software.**

❏ This problem is usually software-related. Try hitting the escape, control-break, or control-C keys.

❏ Try "control-alt-delete" to re-boot the computer.

❏ If you can still not re-boot, try the reset button if the computer has one, or turn the computer off and on again.

❏ The software may not be able to handle the higher speed; try a slower speed and see what happens.

❏ If there is still a problem, use the same steps as for "Computer will not turn on."

# Troubleshooting the Floppy Disk Drive

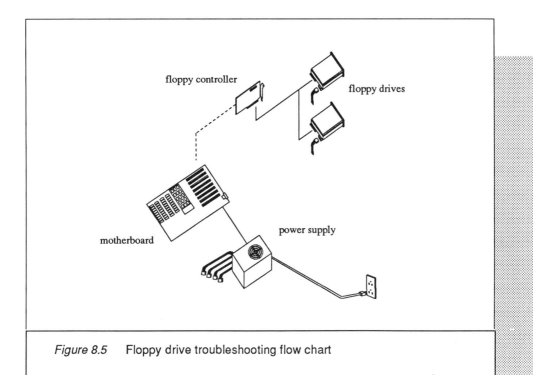

*Figure 8.5*    Floppy drive troubleshooting flow chart

 **Error reading drive.**

❏ Check to be sure there is a disk in the drive and that the drive door is closed.

❏ Try a different disk.

❏ Check to see if the disk is formatted. You may just need to format the disk with DOS format command first.

(WARNING, be sure no important data is on the disk before you try this.)

 **Bad command or file name**

❏ This message indicates an incorrect file name has been entered, try re-entering it with the proper syntax.

 **Boot failure**

❏ Are you trying to "boot" off a nonsystem disk. Insert a disk with DOS and see if it will boot. If it doesn't boot, follow the steps in the next section.

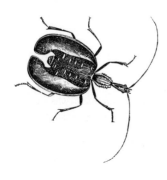

◇(!) **Drive makes noise or doesn't run properly.**

❑ There may be two disks in the drive.

❑ The diskette may be of poor quality and offers too much friction; try a different diskette.

❑ Check whether the label has come off the disk and gotten stuck in the drive.

❑ Check the software. Is the software damaged or is a file missing? Try a new copy of the program.

❑ If one drive is giving problems, change the cables so as to reverse the drives (Drive A becomes drive B and vice versa). Is there still the same problem on the same drive, or has it moved to the other drive?

❑ Try the program on someone else's computer. If it still doesn't work, the problem is probably the software.

❑ Check the drive cables to be sure they are firmly in place.

❑ If the same drive shows the same problem, try replacing the drive.

❑ If the other drive gives problems and the first one is OK, try swapping out the floppy/hard disk controller.

❑ If the problem persists, try swapping the motherboard.

◇(!) **Cannot format a 3 1/2 inch drive for 720 K.**

❑ The "device" or "drive parm" data may have been lost in the config.sys file.

## Troubleshooting the Hard Disk Drive

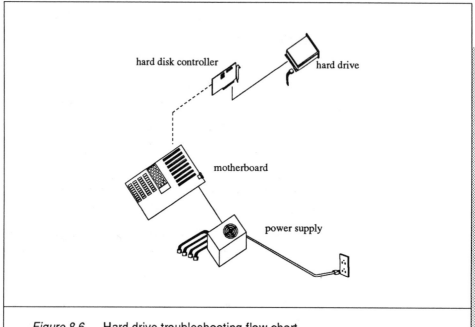

*Figure 8.6*     Hard drive troubleshooting flow chart

 **The hard drive will not boot up when you turn on the computer, or the hard drive makes unusual noise.**

❑ Try booting off drive A and then see if you can access the hard drive. If it is accessible, this means the track zero is bad and the drive needs to be reformatted. It could also mean that the boot up files are corrupted. In this case, recopy the DOS hidden files onto the hard drive with the SYS command, (ie. COPY SYS C:) and then copy the COMMAND.COM file onto the hard drive. If that doesn't work, back up all the data on the drive and reformat the drive.

❑ Open the computer and check that no cables have come loose between the drive and hard disk controller.

❑ If the hard drive is totally inaccessible, you can try reformatting it. This will cause all data to be lost. If you have valuable data on the drive, you can take it to a service center that specializes in hard drives and they may be able to save some of the data.

❑ If the drive will not reformat, try the drive on another computer with the same type of controller (known to be working). If the drive still will not work, replace the drive with a functioning one.

❑ Try another one of the same type of controllers in your computer. If the drive works, replace the faulty controller.

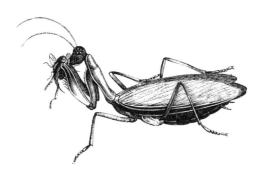

## Troubleshooting the Monitor

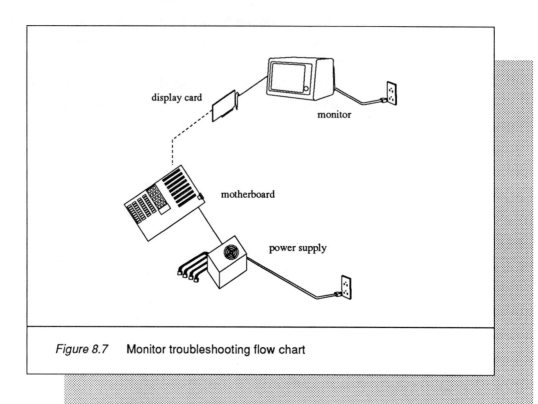

*Figure 8.7*    Monitor troubleshooting flow chart

 **The computer seems to be working, but the screen is blank.**

- ❏ Is the monitor turned on?  Check the green LED "power on" on the monitor if it has one.
- ❏ Adjust the brightness and contrast controls all the way up.
- ❏ Check the video cable from the monitor to the computer to be sure it is properly connected.

❑ Check the wall outlet by plugging in a lamp to see if you have power.

❑ Check the power cable. Is it connected properly at both ends?

❑ Try a different monitor on your computer. If it doesn't work the display card is likely at fault. Replace the display card.

❑ Try your monitor on a different computer. If it doesn't work, replace the monitor or have it repaired by a trained technician.

◊ **Computer boots, but displays "junk" on the screen.**

❑ It may be that the display card is defective; try a different card. If it works, then your first card may be bad.

❑ Try the suspected bad card on another computer. If it displays the same thing, it is fairly conclusive that the card is bad.

◊ **Display is dim, overly bright, or blurry, or unpleasant. Display is off center. Left or right side of monitor is obscured.**

❑ Try adjusting the control knobs located on either the front or the back of the monitor. It may be necessary to open the monitor's casing to get to the proper adjustment controls. In this case be very careful because there are high voltages in the monitor.

◊ **The video display fades and brightens, or is wavy.**

❑ The voltage may be fluctuating due to too many appliances or electric devices on the same branch circuit.

❑ Turn off all other appliances and peripherals, such as printers, external modem, refrigerator, microwave oven, transformers, etc., and see if that solves the problem.

❑ Try a different monitor on your computer; if the problem persists, try swapping out the display card. If the problem was resolved by changing the monitor, repair or replace the monitor.

◊ **Image on the screen is not straight across the screen.**

❑ If the monitor is still under warranty, bring it back to the dealer for adjustment. If you want to do it yourself, bare in mind that this is a potentially dangerous procedure.

WARNING!!! THIS IS A DANGEROUS PROCE-
DURE because it must be done while the monitor is on,
and there are very high voltages around the picture tube.

❑ Open the monitor's casing, and loosen the clamp
holding the coils around the picture tube. You can
loosen them (usually there's a wing nut) and rotate the
coil assembly until the picture straightens.

## Troubleshooting the Keyboard

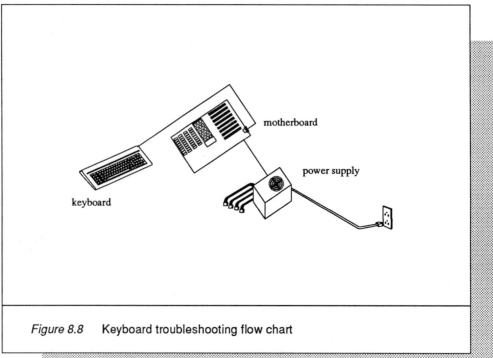

*Figure 8.8*    Keyboard troubleshooting flow chart

 **KB. error, 301 error, or the keyboard is inoperable.**

❑ Make sure the keyboard is plugged in.

❑ Check that the front panel keyboard lock switch is in the unlocked position

❑ If you have an AT/XT switchable keyboard check to see that it is on the proper setting.

❑ Check that no key is stuck.

❏ Try a different keyboard; if it works properly, the original keyboard is suspect.

❏ Try the original keyboard on a different computer. If it doesn't work properly, the keyboard is at fault and needs to be replaced.

⟨!⟩ **You strike the key once and it produces two letters. Striking keys produces no result on screen. Some keys transmit characters and some don't. Wrong Character Set displayed.**

❏ Check the keyboard connector in the back of the computer to make sure it is properly plugged in.

❏ Check that the problem is not software-related by using different software.

❏ Check the Num Lock key to be sure it is not on.

❏ Check for possible stuck keys.

❏ Try a different keyboard.

❏ The switches under the keys tend to wear out from constant use and humidity. Also dirt can get between the contacts, thereby affecting the connections. You can try taking the key tops off and cleaning the contacts with rubbing alcohol.

## Troubleshooting the Memory

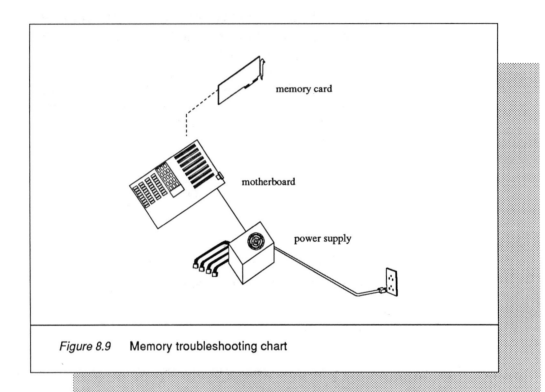

*Figure 8.9*    Memory troubleshooting chart

◊ **Parity errors.**

❑ Parity errors indicate that a memory chip is bad.

❑ First, if the computer has a memory expansion board determine if the faulty chip is on the memory board or the motherboard. If the parity error came up during the RAM check it will stop at the number at which the faulty chip is located. Usually above 640 K or 1 Mb, depending on the motherboard, will be on the memory board.

❑ If the fault is with the memory card, hopefully a RAM chip testing program will have come with the card when you purchased it. This program will locate and often display graphically where the faulty chip is. If you don't have such a program, use the same procedure as outlined below.

❑ It is hard to track down the exact chip which is bad on the motherboard because each BIOS (which sends the error message) for the clone uses a different error message coding. Finding the faulty chips can be a tedious task.

❑ Take out all memory cards.

❑ Try pressing down on all the RAM chips on the motherboard; sometimes corrosion will affect the contacts and cause the parity error. Pressing down on the chips helps seat the chips and improves the connections.

❑ Take out the last bank of chips, and change the DIP switches to reflect any changes in the amount of memory installed (see motherboard documentation).

❑ Do you still have parity errors? If not, you know that the bad chip(s) is one or more of those nine chips. Take out one chip from the remaining installed chips. Replace it one at a time with the nine chips that you just removed. Turn on the computer after installing each chip to see if a parity error pops up. If it does, you know you have found the bad chip. Replace any bad chip(s) with new one(s).

❑ If, after removing the first bank of chips, the computer still has parity problems, remove another bank in the same fashion as previously done until the parity error disappears.  Once you know the bank which contains the faulty chip, do the same individual chip replacement procedure as in the previous step.

## Troubleshooting the Internal Modem

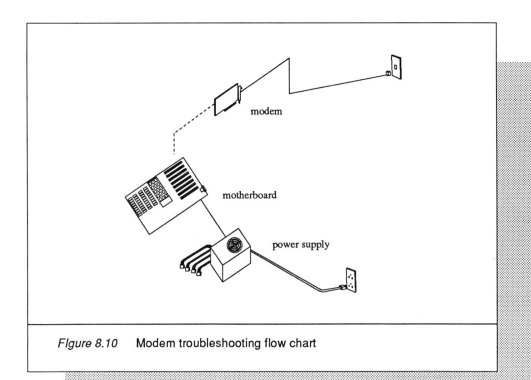

*Figure 8.10*    Modem troubleshooting flow chart

 **Cannot call out or receive calls.**

❏ Make sure the phone line is clear and operable by calling out with a telephone.

❏ Double check that the parameters for baud, parity, stop bits, etc., have been set properly.

❏ Check that the COM ports are matched between the hardware and the communications software.

❑ Check that you have the proper COM port number, DTR setting, and interrupt level settings.

❑ The software may not be functioning properly. Try it on another computer. If it does not work, the software is suspect.

❑ Try other communications software on your computer.

❑ Try taking out or disabling all other serial ports to see if the problem is caused by a COM port, IRQ, or DTR conflict.

❑ Try your modem in another computer, if it does not work there also, the modem is suspect and should be replaced.

❑ Try another modem in your computer.

# Troubleshooting the Serial Mouse

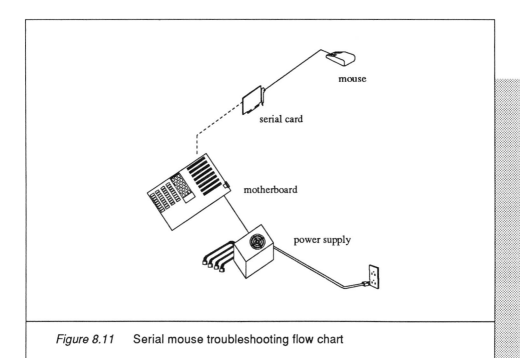

*Figure 8.11*    Serial mouse troubleshooting flow chart

◊⟨!⟩ **Serial mouse does not respond.**

❑ The COM settings, the DTR setting, and possibly the interrupt settings need to be set properly on the serial card. Check with the manual to be sure you have the correct settings.

❑ Remove all other serial ports to be sure they are not conflicting with the mouse.

❏ Try a different mouse on your computer.  If it works, the original mouse is probably faulty and needs to be replaced.

❏ Try the mouse on another computer, if it does not work, the mouse is probably faulty and needs to be replaced.

## Troubleshooting the Printer

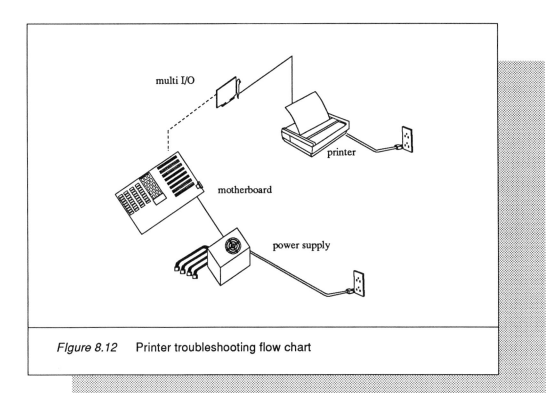

*Figure 8.12*    Printer troubleshooting flow chart

⟨!⟩  **Printer will not print.**

❑  Serial printers can be very problematic. They may
require you to: get a special cable; redirect the
parameters from LPT1 to COM1; and set the baud rate
and parity to match between the software and the
printer. Check with the manufacturer or documentation

for the correct installation procedure. Also, check the following steps as for parallel printer problems.

❏ With the parallel printer, check the connections of the printer cable to the printer and computer.

❏ Check whether the ribbon is worn. Replace it if necessary.

❏ Make sure the printer ribbon is installed correctly.

❏ Try the printer self-test; if it works, go to the next step. If the self test does not work, the problem is printer related.

❏ Try a DOS print screen. This is done by pressing the Shift and Prt Sc keys at the same time. This should print whatever is on your screen. If it works, this means the computer is communicating properly with the printer and it is set up properly.

❏ If you can do a print screen, the installation of your application program is probably incorrect.

❏ If you cannot do a print screen, check that the printer cable is connected to the proper port.

❏ Try a different port.

❏ Try a different card with a different parallel port.

❏ Try removing all other parallel ports to be sure there are no port conflicts. If the printer works, then you know a port conflict exists.

❏ Try the printer on a different computer; if it works, then your computer is at fault. If it still doesn't work, you need to have the printer serviced.

# APPENDICES

# APPENDIX A

# Company Addresses

The following are the names, addresses, and phone numbers of companies mentioned in the text of this book

**Advanced Logic Research, Inc.**
10 Chrysler Rd.
Irvine, CA 92718
(714) 581-6770

**Amdek Corporation**
1901 Zonker Rd.
San Jose, CA 95112
(408) 436-8570

**Advanced Micro Devices (AMD)**
901 Thompson Place
P.O. Box 3453
Sunnyvale, CA 94088
(408) 732-2400

**American Megatrends, Inc.**
4025 Pleasantdale Rd., Ste. 320
Atlanta, GA 30340
(404) 263-8181

**American Micronics, Inc. (AMI)**
17831 Skypark Circle, Suite C
Irvine, CA 92714

**Award Software, Inc.**
130 Knowles Drive
Los Gatos, CA 95030
(408) 370-7979

**AST Research**
2121 Alton Ave.
Irvine, CA 92714
(714) 836-1333

**AT&T**
55 Corporate Drive
Bridgewater, NJ 08807
(800) 922-0354

**Casper Inc.**
3012 Lawrence Expressway
Santa Clara, CA 95051
(408) 922-0188

**Central Point Software Inc.**
9700 SW Capitol Hwy. #100
Portland, OR 97219
(503) 244-5782

**Cerebral Palsy Computer
Access Project**
1904 Franklin #204
Oakland, CA 94562
(415) 832-7430

**Chips and Technologies Inc.**
521 Cottonwood Dr.
Milpitas, CA 95035
(408) 434-0600

**Club American Technologies**
3401 Warren Ave.
Fremont, CA 94539
(415) 490-2201

**Compaq Computer Corp.**
20555 FM 149
Houston, TX 77070
(713) 370-0670

**Cornerstone Technologies, Inc.**
175-A E. Tasman Dr.
San Jose, CA 95134
(408) 433-1600

**Curtis Communications**
1684 Page St.
San Francisco, CA 94117
(415) 626-3549

**Data Technologies Corp.**
2551 Walsh Ave.
Santa Clara, CA 95051
(408) 727-8899

**Dell Computer Corp.**
9505 Arboretom Blvd.
Austin, TX 78754
(800) 274-3355

**DEST Corp.**
1201 Cadillac Crt.
Milpitas, CA 95035
(800) 538-7582
(408) 946-7100

**DTK**
Eltech Research, Inc.
1725 McCandless Drive
Milipitas, CA 95035
(408) 942-0990

**Enabling Technologies Inc.**
600 S. Dearborn St., St. 1307
Chicago, IL 60605
(313) 427-0386

**Epson America**
2780 Lomita Blvd.
Torrence, CA 90505
(213) 539-9140

**Everex Systems, Inc.**
48431 Milmont Drive
Fremont, CA 94538
(415) 498-1111

**Five Star Computers**
3220 Commander, Ste.102
Carrollton, TX 75006
(800) 752-5555

**Fujitsu**
3055 Orchard Dr.
San Jose, CA 95134-2317
(800) 626-46 86

**Genoa Systems Corp.**
73E Trimble Road
San Jose, CA 95131
(408) 432-9090

**Garrison Software**
P.O. Box 70386
Bellvue, WA 98007
(800) 368-4555

**Hayes Micro Computer Prod.**
705 Westeck Dr.
Norcross, GA 30092

**Hercules Technology**
921 Parker St.
Berkeley, CA 94710
(415) 540-6000

**Harold Henderson**
Writing Consultant
119 Laurel Lane
Austin, TX 78705
(512) 472-5828

**Hewlett Packard**
3000 Hanover
Palo Alto, CA 94304
(800) 367-4772

**Intel Corp.**
PCEO
5200 Neelam Young Parkway
Hillsboro, OR 97124
(800) 538-3373

**Kaypro Corp.**
533 Stevens Ave.
Solano Beach, CA 92075
(619)481-4300

**Landmark Software**
1142 Pomegranate Court
Sunnyvale, CA 94087
(408) 733-4035

**Laser Connection**
P. O. Box 850296
Mobile, AL 36685
(205) 633-7223

**Lotus Development Corp.**
55 Cambridge Parkway
Cambridge, MA 02142
(617) 577-8500

**Maxi-Switch Co.**
9697 East River Rd.
Minneapolis, Mn. 55433
(616) 755-7660

**Meridian Technology, Inc.**
7 Corporate Park Suite 100
Irvine, CA 92714
(714) 261-1199

**Microsoft Corp.**
16011 NE 36th Way
Redmond, WA 98073
(206) 882-8080

**MiniScribe Corporation**
1861 Lefthand Circle
Longmont, CO 80501
(303) 651-6000

**Mitsuba Electronics America, Inc.**
991 Knox St.
Torrance, CA 90502
(800) 556-1234

**Mitsubishi Electronics**
991 Knox St.
Torrance, CA 90502
(213) 515-3993

**Modular Information Systems**
431 Ashbury Street
San Francisco, CA 94117
(415) 552-8648

**NEC**
1255 Michael Drive
Wood Dale, IL 60191-1094
(312) 860-9500

**Omura Illustrations**
829 Pomona Ave.
Albany, CA 94706
(415) 523-1113

**PC Pursuit-GTE Sprint**
(800) TELENET

**Paradise Systems, Inc.**
99 South Hill Drive
Brisbane, CA 94005
(415) 468-6692

**Peter Norton Computing, Inc.**
2210 Wilshire Blvd, Ste. 186
Santa Monica, CA 90603
(213) 453-2361

**Personal Computer Support Group**
11035 Harry Hines Blvd. #207
Dallas, TX 75229
(214) 351-0564

**Phoenix Technologies**
320 Norwood Park South
Norwood, MA 02062
(617) 769-7020

**Portillo Kester Photography**
765 Minna
San Francisco, CA 94103
(415) 285-2455

**Powerlight Systems**
46 Crane Ct.
Alameda, CA 94501
(415) 523-1139

**Practical Peripherals**
31245 La Baya Dr.
Westlake, CA 91362
(818) 991-8200

**Princeton Graphics**
170 Wall St.
Princeton, NJ 08540

**Publishers Group West**
5856 Doyle Street
Emeryville, CA 94608
(415) 658-3453

**QIC Research, Inc.**
753 Ames Ave.
Milpitas, CA 95035
(800) 843-0806
(408) 942-8086 in CA

**Quadram Corp.**
One Quad Way
Norcross, GA 30093
(404) 923-6666

**Samsung Electronic Devices**
16031 S. Carmenita Rd.
Cerritos, CA 90701
(213) 404-1835

**Seagate Technology**
920 Disc Dr.
Scotts Valley, CA 95066
(800) 468-3472

**Sigma Designs, Inc.**
46501 Landing Parkway
Fremont, CA 94538
(415) 770-0100

**S.F. Micro**
1825 Lombard St.
San Francisco, CA 94123
(415) 929-1505

**Software Masters**
6352 N. Guilford Ave.
Indianapolis, IN 46220
(317) 253-8088

**Sony Corporation of America**
Sony Drive
Park Ridge, NJ 0765
(201) 930-1000

**Storage Dimensions, Inc.**
2145 Hamilton Ave
San Jose, CA 95125
(408) 987-0300

**Storage Systems Engineering**
3350 Scotts Blvd., Suite 1902
Santa Clara, CA 95054
(408) 727-6040

**Sunteck Information Systems**
5369 Randall Place
Fremont, CA 94538
(415) 657-0567

**Tandy Corporation/Radio Shack**
1800 One Tandy Center
Fort Worth, TX 76102
(817) 390-2728

**Teac Corporation of America**
7733 Telegraph Road
Montebello, CA 90640
(213) 726-0303

**Team Technologies, Inc.**
19205 Parthenia, Ste. J
Northridge, CA 91324
(818) 886-9726

**Toshiba America, Inc.**
9740 Irvine Blvd.
Irvine, CA 92718
(717) 380-3000

**To the Point Graphics**
San Francisco, CA
(415) 931-3765

**Thomson International Systems**
5731 W. Slawson Ave.
Culver City, CA 90230
(213) 568-1002

**Ventura Publisher (see Xerox)**

**Video Seven Inc.**
46335 Landing Parkway
Fremont, CA 94538
(415) 656-7800

**Moniterm Corp.**
5740 Green Circle Dr.
Minnetonka, MN 55343
(612) 935-4151

**Western Digital Corp.**
2445 McCabe Way
Irvine, CA 92714
(714) 863-0102

**Whole Earth Access Computers**
2940 7th Street
Berkeley, CA 94710
(415) 653-7758

**WordPerfect Corp.**
288 West Center Street
Orem, UT 84057
(801) 227-4020

**Wyse Technology**
3571 North First St.
San Jose, CA 95134
(800) 438-9973

**Xerox Corp.**
1301 Ridgeview Dr.
Mailstop 179
Lewisville, TX 75067
(800) 822-8221

# APPENDIX B

# Computer Magazines

## Major National Computer Magazines

The following is a list of national computer magazines along with phone numbers for subscription information.

**Byte**
One Phoenix Mill Lane
Peterborough, NH 03458
(603) 924-9281

A monthly magazine targeted for the user who wants a technical understanding of the computer. The articles are quite technical, with in depth product reviews, and a sleek presentation.

**Computer Shopper**
Patch Publications
5211 S. Washington Ave.
Titusville, FL 32780
(800) 372-9926
(305) 269-3211 in FL

A monthly magazine which uses a tabloid format and contains lots of ads for PC clones and parts; it is especially good for the bargain hunter. Has a very comprehensive national list of computer bulletin boards, user groups, and computer shows.

## Family Computing and Home Office

730 Broadway
New York, NY 10003
(212) 505-3585

A monthly magazine featuring articles on start up businesses in the home, The articles are informative, "inspiring," and easy to read.

## Infoworld

1060 Marsh Road, Suite C-200
Menlo Park, CA 94025
(818) 577-7233

A weekly magazine directed at the corporate user. Free to those who qualify. Contains the latest product reviews, rumors, and articles.

## Nuts & Volts

P.O. Box 1111
Placentia, CA 92670
(714) 632-7721

This is a monthly electronics parts magazine which has clone advertisements and a calendar of events listing of computer swaps.

## PC Clones

5211 S. Washington Ave.
Titusville, FL 32780
(305) 269-1663
(800) 327-9926

A monthly magazine specifically for PC clones. Contains many clone advertisements.

## PC Magazine

P. O. Box 2445
Boulder, CO 80322
(800) 525-0643

One of the major monthly computer magazines. Has a general nontechnical appeal and uses a sleek presentation. Contains as many as 500 pages of advertisements, product reviews and articles; the reviews are, however, not very critical.

## PC Week

P.O. Box 5970
Cherry Hill, NJ 08034
(609) 428-5000

A weekly sleek magazine directed at the corporate computer user. Not available on news stands, but free to qualified users, otherwise $120 per year. Very informative with many product reviews and good articles.

## PC World
501 Second St.
San Francisco, CA 94107
(415) 546-7722

A monthly magazine with sleek but not overly technical presentation. It has an award winning design and contains many comprehensive product reviews and articles.

## PC Resource
80 Elm St.
Peterborough, NH 03458
(800) 441-4403

A monthly magazine with many useful and easy to understand "hands on" type of articles

geared toward the PC clone owner.

## Personal Computing
10 Mulholland Dr.
Hasbrouck Heights, NJ 07604
(800) 525-0643

A monthly magazine which emphasizes software.

## Soft Sector
P. O. Box 385
Prospect, KY 40059
(502) 228-4492
A monthly magazine with an emphasis on IBM compatible computers. This magazine used to focus on the Sanyo 550 computer. It contains articles and reviews.

# Regional Computer Magazines

The magazines listed here are usually in a tabloid format and given away free. They are regionally based and contain local advertisements.

**Baltimore Computer Digest**
 10451 Mill Run Circle St.400
 Owings Mills, MD 21117
 (301) 583-6039

**California Computer News**
 1831 V Street
 Sacramento, CA 95818
 (916) 443-7163

**Capitol Computer Digest**
 1408 N. Fillmore St., Suite 1
 Arlington, Virginia 22201
 (703) 525-7900

**Computer and Business
Equipment Review**
 P.O. Box 1027
 Scottsdale, AZ 85252-1027
 (602) 946-5005

**Computer Currents**
 P.O. Box 2339
 Berkeley, CA 94702
 (415) 848-6860

**Computer Living New York**
 5793 Tyndall Ave.
 Riverdale, NY 10471
 (212) 601-2832

**Computer News of San Diego**
 3945 Camino Del Rio, Ste 304
 San Diego, CA 92108
 (619) 284-6000

**Computerpeople**
 700 N. Green St., Suite 504
 Chicago, IL 60622
 (312) 829-3505

**Microtimes**
 5951 Canning St.
 Oakland, CA 94609
 (415) 652-3810

**Minneapolis Computer User**
 12 S. 6th, Suite 1030
 Minneapolis, MN 55402
 (612) 339-7571

**Puget Sound Computer User**
2724 N.E. 45th St. #385
Seattle, WA 98105
(206) 547-4950

**St. Louis Computing**
1300 Hampton, Suite 117
St. Louis, MO 63139-3189
(314) 644-5854

**Texas Computing**
17818 Davenport, Suite 119
Dallas, TX 75252
(214) 931-0157

# APPENDIX C

# Computer Show and Swap Promoters

The following list is of computer show and swap meet promoters, and the cities in which they exhibit. You can look up the city nearest you and call or write the promoter for the dates and times of their next shows.

**American Business Equipment and Computer Trade Show**
Key Productions
234 Murphy Rd.
Hartford, CT 06114
(203) 247-8363

Hartford, CT
Boston, MA

**Computer/Camera/Video Swap Meet**
P. O. Box 1551
Mishawaka, IN 46544
(219) 259-2968

South Bend, IN

**Computer Central Multi-Vendor PC Show**
P. O. Box 529
Dearfield, IL 60015
(312) 940-7547

Chicago, IL
Itasca, IL

**Class Productions Inc.**
4207 N. Clinton St.
Fort Wayne, IN 46805
(219) 483-6144

Indianapolis, IN
St Louis, MO
Cincinnati, OH

Columbus, OH
Dayton, OH

## Computerama USA
20219 Mack Ave.
Grosse Pointe Wds, MI 48236
(313) 884-2243
Los Angeles,CA

Rosemont, IL
Minneapolis, MN
Buffalo, NY
Cleveland, OH
Columbus, OH

## Coastal Marketing Corporation
9 Whistlestop Mall
Rockport, MA 01966
(617) 546-3475

Hyannis, MA
Methuen, MA
Natick, MA
North Dartmouth, MA
Peabody, MA
Portland, ME
Warwick, RI

## Computer Trading Post
511 West Glen Oaks #228
Glendale, CA 91202
(818) 352-9829

Glendale, CA

## Electronics & Computer Expo
Great Southern Shows
1222 Shackleton Road
Jacksonville, FL 32211
(904) 743-8000

Jacksonville, FL
Orlando, FL

## Golden Gate Shows
P. O. Box 587
Corte Madera, CA 94925
(415) 388-8893

Burbank, CA
Oakland, CA
Sacramento, CA
San Diego, CA
San Bernardino, CA
Santa Rosa, CA
Vallejo, CA
Ventura, CA
Portland, OR
Las Vegas, NV
Salt Lake City, UT
Seattle, WA

## Great Southern Shows
1222 Shackleton Road
Jacksonville, Florida 32211
(904) 743-8000

Jacksonville, FL
Orlando, FL

## Interface Group

300 First Avenue
Needham, MA 02194
(617) 449-6953
(617) 449-6600

San Francisco, CA
Atlanta , GA  (COMDEX)
Boston, MA
Las Vegas, NV (COMDEX)

## Ken Gordon Productions, Inc.

P. O. Box 13
Franklin Park, NJ 08823
(201) 297-2526
(800) 631-0062

Bridgeport, CT
Boxborough, MA
Woburn, MA
New Carrollton, MD
Parsippany, NJ
Secaucus, NJ
Wayne, NJ
Hempstead, NY
Valley Forge, PA
Willow Grove, PA

## Midwest Computer Shows

6N351 Keeney Road
Roselle, Il 60172
1-800-443-8693

Wheaton, Il

## Micro Shows

1209 Donnelly Ave., Suite 203
Burlingame, CA 94010
(408) 649-3624

Santa Clara, CA
San Francisco, CA
San Jose, CA
San Mateo, CA

## National Computer Conference (NCC)

1899 Preston White Dr.
Reston, VA 22091
(800) NCC-1987

Chicago, Il

## PC Expo

P.O. Box 1026
Englewood Cliffs, NJ 07632
(201) 569-8542

Chicago, IL
New York, NY

## RK Productions

P. O. Box 18906
San Jose, CA 95158
(408) 978-7927
(800) 252-7927

Del Mar, CA
Costa Mesa, CA
Orange County, CA
Pomona, CA
San Mateo, CA

San Diego, CA
San Jose, CA
Denver, CO
Cherry Hill, NJ
Philadelphia, PA

## Radix Enterprises
P. O. Box 774
Christiansburg, VA 24074
(703) 763-3736

Roanoke, VA

## Trenton Computer Festival
Trenton State College
Hillwood Lakes CN4700
Trenton, NJ 08650-4700
(609) 771-2487

Trenton, NJ

## Tri State Computer Fairs
P. O. Box 76
Livingston, NJ 07939
(201) 553-1991
New Castle, DE
Silver Spring, MD
Cherry Hill, NJ
Secaucus, NJ
Albany, NY
Suffern, NY
Pittsburg, PA

# APPENDIX D

# IBM Diagnostic Error Codes

The error codes listed here are the IBM error codes. Some or all are used by IBM clone computer manufacturers.

| Code | Description |
|------|-------------|
| **101** | Main system board failed |
| **109** | Direct memory access test error |
| **121** | Unexpected hardware interrupts occurred |
| **131** | Cassette wrap test failed |
| **199** | User indicated configuration not correct |
| **201** | Memory test failed |
| **301** | Keyboard did not respond to software reset correctly or a stuck key failure was detected. If a stuck key was detected, the scan code for the key is displayed |
| **302** | User indicated error from the keyboard test |
| **401** | Monochrome memory test, horizontal sync frequency test, or video test failed |
| **408** | User indicated display attributes failure |

**416**   User indicated character set failure

**424**   User indicated 80X25 mode failure

**432**   Parallel port test failed (monochrome adapter)

**501**   Color memory test failed, horizontal sync frequency test, or video test failed

**508**   User indicated display attribute failure

**516**   User indicated character set failure

**524**   User indicated 80x25 mode failure

**532**   User indicated 40x25 mode failure

**540**   User indicated 320x200 graphics mode failure

**548**   User indicated 640x200 graphics mode failure

**601**   Diskette power on diagnostics test failed

**602**   Diskette test failed

**606**   Diskette verify function failed

**607**   Write protected diskette

**608**   Bad command diskette status returned

**610**   Diskette initialization failed

**611**   Timeout - diskette status returned

**612**   Bad NEC - diskette status returned

**613**   Bad DMA - diskette status returned

**621**   Bad seek - diskette status returned

**622**   Bad CRC - diskette status returned

**623**   Record not found - diskette status returned

**624**   Bad address mark - diskette status returned

**625**   Bad NEC seek - diskette status returned

**626**   Diskette data compare error

**7xx**   8087 math coprocessor

**901**   Parallel printer adapter test failed

**10xx**   Reserved for parallel printer adapter

**1101**   Asynchronous communications adapter test failed

**1201** Alternate Asynchronous communications adapter test failed

**1301** Game control adapter test failed

**1302** Joystick test failed

**1401** Printer test failed

**15xx** Sdlc communications adapter errors

**1510** 8255 port B failure

**1511** 8255 port A failure

**1512** 8255 prot C failure

**1513** 8253 timer 1 did not reach terminal count

**1514** 8253 timer 1 stuck on

**1515** 8253 timer 0 did not reach terminal count

**1516** 8253 timer 0 stuck on

**1517** 8253 timer 2 did not reach terminal count

**1518** 8253 timer 2 stuck on

**1519** 8273 port B error

**1520** 8273 port A error

**1521** 8273 command/read timeout

**1522** Interrupt level 4 failure

**1523** Ring Indicate stuck on

**1524** Receive clock stuck on

**1525** Transmit clock stuck on

**1526** Test indicate stuck on

**1527** Ring indicate not on

**1528** Receive clock not on

**1529** Transmit clock not on

**1530** Test indicate not on

**1531** Data set ready not on

**1532** Carrier detect not on

**1533** Clear to send not on

**1534** Data set ready stuck on

**1536** Clear to send stuck on

**1537** Level 3 interrupt failure

**1538** Receive interrupt results error

**1539** Wrap data miscompare

**1540** DMA channel 1 error

**1541** DMA channel 1 error

**1542** Error in 8273 error checking or status reporting

**1547** Stray interrupt level 4

**1548** Stray interrupt level 3

**1549** Interrupt presentation sequence timeout

**17xx** Fixed Disk errors

**1701** Fixed disk Post error

**1702** Fixed disk adapter error

**1703** Fixed disk drive error

**1704** Fixed disk adapter or drive error

**18xx** I/O Expansion unit errors

**1801** I/O Expansion unit POST error

**1810** Enable/Disable failure

**1811** Extender card wrap test failed (disabled)

**1812** High order address lines failure (disabled)

**1813** Wait state failure (disabled)

**1814** Enable/Disable could not be set on

**1815** Wait state failure (enabled)

**1816** Extender card wrap test failed (enabled)

**1817** High order address lines failure (enabled)

**1818** Disable not functioning

**1819** Wait request switch not set correctly

**1820** Receiver card wrap test failure

**1821** Receiver high order address lines failure

**20xx** Bisync communications adapter errors

**2010** 8255 port a failure

**2011** 8255 port b failure

**2012** 8255 port c failure

**2013** 8253 timer 1 did not reach terminal count

**2014** 8253 timer 1 stuck on

**2016** 8253 timer 2 did not reach terminal count or timer 2 stuck on

**2017** 8251 Data set ready failed to come on

**2018** 8251 Clear to send not sensed

**2019** 8251 Data set ready stuck on

**2020** 8251 Clear to send stuck on

**2021** 8251 hardware reset failed

**2022** 8251 software reset failed

**2023** 8251 software "error reset" failed

**2024** 8251 transmit ready did not come on

**2025** 8251 receive ready did not come on

**2026** 8251 could not force "overrun" error status

**2027** Interrupt failure-no timer interrupt

**2028** Interrupt failure-transmit, replace card or planar

**2029** Interrupt failure-transmit, replace card

**2030** Interrupt failure-receive, replace card or planar

**2031** Interrupt failure-receive, replace card

**2033** Ring indicate stuck on

**2034** Receive clock stuck on

**2035** Transmit clock stuck on

**2036** Test indicate stuck on

**2037** Ring indicate stuck on

**2038** Receive clock not on

**2039** Transmit clock not on

**2040** Test indicate not on

**2041** Data set ready not on

**2042** Carrier detect not on

**2043** Clear to send not on

**2044** Data set ready stuck on

**2045** Carrier detect stuck on

**2046** Clear to send stuck on

**2047** Unexpected transmit interrupt

**2048** Unexpected receive interrupt

**2049** Transmit data did not equal receive data

**2050** 8251 detected overrun error

**2051** Lost data set ready during data wrap

**2052** Receive timeout during data wrap

**2110** 8255 port a failure

**2111** 8255 port b failure

**2112** 8255 port c failure

**2113** 8253 timer 1 did not reach terminal count

**2114** 8253 timer 1 stuck on

**2116** 8253 timer 2 did not reach terminal count or

**2117** 8251 Date set ready failed to come on

**2117** 8251 Clear to send not sensed

**2118** 8251 Data set ready stuck on

**2119** 8251 Clear to send stuck on

**2120** 8251 hardware reset failed

**2121** 8251 software reset failed

**2122** 8251 software "error reset" failed

**2123** 8251 transmit ready did not come on

**2124** 8251 receive ready did not come on

**2125** 8251 could not force "overrun" error status

**2126** Interrupt failure-no timer interrupt

**2128** Interrupt failure-transmit, replace card or

**2129** Interrupt failure-transmit, replace card

**2130** Interrupt failure-receive, replace card or planar

**2131** Interrupt failure-receive, replace card

**2133** Ring indicate stuck on

**2134** Receive clock stuck on

**2135** Transmit clock stuck on

**2136** Test indicate stuck on

**2137** Ring indicate stuck on

**2138** Receive clock not on

**2139** Transmit clock not on

**2140** Test indicate not on

**2142** Data set ready not on

**2142** Carrier detect not on

**2143** Clear to send not on

**2144** Data set ready stuck on

**2145** Carrier detect stuck on

**2146** Clear to send stuck on

**2147** Unexpected transmit interrupt

**2148** Unexpected receive interrupt

**2149** Transmit data did not equal receive data

**2150** 8251 detected overrun error

**2151** Lost data set ready during data wrap

**2152** Receive timeout during data wrap

# GLOSSARY

**8088**  This chip is an Intel manufactured microprocessor used in the PC, XT, compatibles, and clones.  It processes data 16-bits at a time internally but communicates with the outside world 8-bits at a time.

**8086**  This microprocessor chip has the same internal structure as the 8088 chip except that it has a true 16-bit data path.  It is used in some XT compatibles like the AT&T 6300 and some laptops as well as the IBM PS/2 Models 25 and 30.

**80286**  This chip is the second generation of Intel produced microprocessors and is used as the CPU of the IBM AT, clones and compatibles as well as the IBM PS/2 Models 50 and 60.

**80386**  This CPU chip is the third generation of Intel made microprocessor chips for microcomputers and is used in the IBM PS/2 Models 70 and 80.  This chip processes data 32-bits at a time (the same as most large and powerful mainframe computers) and communicates with the outside world at 32-bits.

**80486**  This is the fourth generation of Intel made CPU chip which is still in development.  It is said to still be a 32-bit chip but is 3 to 5 times faster than the 386.

**80287**  This is a math coprocessor chip which works in conjunction with the 80286 and is added to speed up the processing of mathematical calculations.

**Access Time**  The amount of time it takes the computer to read data from RAM or hard disk, measured in nanoseconds and milliseconds respectively.

**Add-on**  A card or device attached internally to the computer to increase its capabilities.  Some examples would be a memory board, an internal modem, and a floppy drive.

**Analog**  An electrical signal which can have any voltage value. With regards to monitors, the output of a VGA card is an analog signal as opposed to a digital signal which is used in EGA or monochrome cards.

**Apple DOS**  An operating system used on the Apple II series of computers.

**Application Software**  A program that performs specific functions on the computer, such as word processing, database, telecommunication, and spreadsheet applications.

**Architecture**  The overall design or structure of a microprocessor.

**Artificial Intelligence (AI)**  Software which attempts to imitate certain intellectual capabilities of humans such as reasoning, adapting, or learning.

**Asynchronous**  The transmission of data one bit at a time.

**Autoanswer**  A feature on some modems for automatically answering and responding to incoming calls.

**Autodial**  A feature on some modems for automatically dialing a telephone number.

**Passive Backplane**  A concept where the CPU and all the associated components are placed on an expansion card instead of a motherboard. This card then plugs into a series of expansion slots.

**Backup**  A spare copy of your program or data.  Usually the original software disks are backed up so that if they are damaged you will not lose the software.  Also all data should be backed up in case the original disk becomes damaged.

**Bank**  A row of nine RAM chips.

**Bare Bones**  A common expression to signify the minimum configuration required to form a basic computer system.

**Base Memory** The first 640 K of memory in an IBM type of computer under DOS.

**BASIC** (Beginner's All-purpose Symbolic Instruction Code) This is a common programming language and comes on a set of ROM in IBM PC, XT, AT computers. A version referred to as GW BASIC (GW supposedly for Gee Whiz) is widely available on disk.

**Baud** This is a measurement of speed in bits per second over a serial line. Most modems, for example, operate at 300, 1200, or 2400 baud. Direct serial connections can operate at baud rates up to 19200.

**Bell 212A** A communications protocol standard developed by Bell laboratories.

**BIOS (Basic Input/Output System)** The most basic software code used to controls the operations of the computer. The BIOS is a software program which resides in a chip referred to as a ROM.

**Bit** Short for "binary digit," is the most elementary unit of information. A bit consist of an electrical voltage that is either on or off (also referred to as a 1 or 0).

**Board** Refers to a printed circuit board used in the computer, such as expansion cards.

**Booting** The startup procedure of the computer when it is first turned on and the vital parts of DOS are loaded into memory.

**Bug** Refers to a problem in either hardware or software.

**Bulletin Board Service (BBS)** An online database which can be accessed by others who have a computer and modem.

**Bus** The electrical roadway between the CPU and all other parts of the computer. The 8088-based computers use an 8 bit bus and the 286 computers use a 16 bit bus.

**Byte**  Each byte consist of 8 bits and represents a character such as a letter, number, or symbol.

**Cache Memory**  A RAM buffer used to store data for fast access.  The two most common types are disk caching and CPU to a fast RAM caching.

**Card**  Same as board. It refers to a printed circuit board used to expand the computer.

**CDROM  (Compact Disk Read Only Memory)**  A storage medium where digital data is stored on a laser disk.  The advantage is the ability to store large amounts of data (up to 11 gigabytes).

**Central Processing Unit (CPU)**  Same as a microprocessor.  The 8088, 80286, and 68000 are the CPU's of the XT, AT, and Macintosh respectively.

**Centronics port**  Same as parallel port, it is for the transmission of 8 bits of data at a time. It has become the standard for connecting printers to the computer.

**Character**  A number, letter, or symbol seen by the computer as consisting of eight bits or one byte.

**Chip**  Colloquial name for an integrated circuit which is etched into a piece of silicon.  It consists of a large number of tiny transistors, diodes, and other components.

**Clock**  There are two different types of time devices in the computer.  One sets the speed of the computers operation.  The other is operated by a battery and keeps track of the time and date.

**Clone**  A direct hardware copy of an IBM computer.

**CMOS**  Stands for Complementary Metal Oxide Silicon, and is an advanced technology in chip manufacturing. The net advantage is much lower power consumption but it has one drawback of being more expensive than its counterpart, NMOS.

**Cold Boot** Refers to booting the computer by turning on the power switch.

**COM1, COM2, etc.** The terms given by MS/PC-DOS to the different serial ports.

**Configuring** The process of setting the configuration parameters via the setup menu.

**Compatible** A computer which will run all the IBM standard software but is not totally hardware interchangeable with an IBM computer.

**Compatibility** Refers to the ability of hardware and software to work together with other hardware and software without problems. Products not functioning together are referred to as incompatible

**Configuration** The specific combination of parts that makes up a computer system.

**Configuration Software** Software specifically written for 286 and 386-based computers to tell the computer what specific combination of parts have been installed. This data is stored in a battery backed chip on the motherboard.

**Controller** A circuit board that acts as an interface between the motherboard and a floppy or hard drive.

**Coprocessor** This type of chip is designed to assist the CPU with certain tasks. Examples are math coprocessors for mathematical functions and graphics coprocessors for graphics functions.

**CP/M** Stands for Control Program/Monitor and like MS/PC DOS is a software operating system.

**CPU** See Central Processing Unit.

**Cursor** A little blinking rectangular spot on the computer screen that shows where the next character you type will be placed.

**Data**  Information stored in digital or binary form.

**Data Base**  A computerized compilation of information organized by various categories such as name, address, city, state, zip code, telephone number, etc.  The leading data base software for the IBM standard is dBase by Ashton Tate.

**Default**  A recommended or predetermined choice in a program.

**Diagnostic Diskette**  A floppy disk containing diagnostic or troubleshooting software.

**Digital**  The use of specific voltage levels to represent data and information. (See Analog.)

**DIP Switch**  An abbreviation of "Dual In-line Package Switch," a kind of switch used to configure the computer and usually found on the motherboard.

**Disk**  A flat magnetic medium used for the permanent storage of information.

**Disk Operating System (DOS)**  A software program used to do general housekeeping chores.  These include CP/M, MS-DOS, PC-DOS, Unix, OS/2, Xenix, etc.

**Downward Compatible**  The ability of new generations of computers to use hardware and software designed for previous generations of computers.

**DRAM (Dynamic Random Access Memory)**  A chip used for the temporary storage of computer data.

**Drive**  A mechanical device for the permanent storage of information, such as a floppy or hard drive.

**EEMS (Expanded Extended Memory Specification)** A software scheme designed by AST, Quadram, and Ashton-Tate to allow DOS to access memory above 640 K.

**EMS** (Expanded Memory Specification) A software scheme designed by Intel, Lotus, and Microsoft to allow XT, AT, 386 computers to use memory above 640 K with DOS.

**EMS 4.0** A software scheme which is a combination of EMS and EEMS.

**EPROM (Erasable programmable read only memory)** A chip onto which software may be written. The contents may be erased by removing a protective seal and exposing the chip to ultraviolet light, a new program may then be written onto the chip.

**Ergonomics** The science of designing machinery for efficient human use.

**Expansion Boards** Used to add features such as memory, hard drives and other components to the computer. They generally fit into slots on the motherboard.

**Expansion Slot** A slot in the computer for adding expansion cards. For instance the XT contains eight expansion slots.

**Extended Memory** The memory beyond the first 640 K of RAM on the 286 or 386-based computer when DOS is used.

**Firmware** A program which is permanently embedded into a ROM chip. It functions the same way as software but is essentially a piece of hardware.

**Fixed Disk** See hard drive.

**Floppy Diskette** A thin magnetically coated disk of mylar encased in a plastic jacket used for storing data. The two most popular formats are 5 1/4 inch and 3 1/2 inch.

**Floppy Disk Drive** A device used for reading and writing data to a floppy diskette. There are two commonly used sizes, the 5 1/4 inch and 3 1/2 inch drives.

**Floppy Disk Controller** A card which controls the operation of a floppy disk drive.

**Full Length Card** An expansion card which fills the entire length of the computer.

**Fully Configured** A computer with all the basic parts required for a functioning system.

**Function Keys** These are special keys on a keyboard programmed for a specific operation; they are designated with an F1, F2, F3, etc.

**Game Port** A 9 pin connector, generally on the back of the computer, for connecting a joy stick, paddles, etc.

**Gigabytes** A unit of computer memory measurement, it is equivalent to one billion bytes or characters.

**Half Length Card** Also called a short card. An expansion card which does not fill the entire length of the chassis.

**Hard Card** A hard drive mounted vertically on a card together with its controller.

**Hard Disk Drive** A set of magnetic plates, permanently encased in a metal enclosure, on which data is stored; it has faster access time and greater storage capabilities than floppy disk drives.

**Hardware** The physical part of a computer such as monitor, keyboard, case, etc.

**Hayes Compatible** Refers to modems which support the Hayes command set.

**I/O** See both Input and Output.

**Input**  Data coming into the computer from sources such as the keyboard, a mouse, digitizing pad, drives, etc.

**Integrated Circuits (ICs)**  A general term for all computer chips.

**Interface**  An intermediary link allowing two devices to be connected.

**Joystick**  A mechanical device with a lever used primarily for games.

**Jumper**  Consists of shorting pins which enable or disable certain functions on an electrical device.

**Keyboard**  An input device containing keys with letters and numbers for entering information into the computer.

**Kilobyte (K)**  A unit of computer memory measurement, it equals 1024 bytes.

**LEDs**  Stands for light-emitting diodes and are little lights often used as indicator lights on the computer's front panel to indicate power on, hard drive on, etc.

**Load**   To transfer a software program from the disk into random access memory.

**Local Area Network (LAN)**  The short distance connection of computers for the sharing of information and peripherals.  Often used in an office environment.

**LPT1, LPT2, LPT3**  The terms assigned by MS/PC-DOS to the parallel ports.

**Mainframe**  Is a very large computer with more powerful processing capabilities than a minicomputer or microcomputer.

**Megabyte (M, Mb, or Meg)**   A unit of computer memory measurement, it equals 1,000,000 bytes.

**Megahertz (MHz)**  A unit of frequency measurement.  One hertz equals one cycle per second.

**Menu**  A list of selections displayed on the computer screen from which to choose.

**Memory**  A broad term for the different forms of storing information in the computer;  ie., RAM, ROM, floppy disk, hard disk, tape, etc.

**Memory Board**  An expansion card containing RAM chips.  It is used to increase the computer's memory.

**Memory Caching**  A memory scheme that uses a small amount of fast memory along with slower memory to speed up the operation of the computer.

**MHz**  Abbreviation for Megahertz.

**Micro Channel**  The bus design used on the IBM PS/2 Models 50, 60, and 80 computers.

**Microprocessor**  Also referred to as the central processing unit (CPU), it is the brain of the computer,

**Microcomputer**  A small computer, usually small enough to fit on a desk.

**Minicomputer**  A computer between the size and capabilities of a microcomputer and a mainframe.

**Modem**  Short for **modular/demo**dulator.  Used to transmit digital signals over telephone lines by first converting them in to analog form and then reconverting them back to digital signals at the other end of the line.

**Monitor**  A device used to display computer generated images on a CRT screen.

**Monochrome Display**  A term which describe s a monitor that is capable of displaying only one color or shades of one color.

**Motherboard** The main circuit board containing the CPU, expansion slots, main memory, and other essential components.

**MS-DOS** A 16-bit operating system written by Microsoft Inc. and used in IBM-standard computers.

**Multiple Input/Output card** Also known as a Multi I/O card. A card containing various combinations of serial, parallel, and games ports.

**Multitasking** The ability of the computer to do several tasks at the same time.

**MultiScan Monitor** A type of monitor capable of being used with a wide variety of display cards.

**Multiuser** The ability for several remote computers to access information on one computer called the file server.

**Nanosecond** A measurement of time used to rate the speed of RAM chips. It equals one billionth of a second.

**Network** See LAN and Multiuser.

**Numeric Keypad** A part of the keyboard used for the rapid entry of numbers. Usually found on the far right side of the keyboard.

**Off-The-Shelf Components** Components which are manufactured by several companies and readily available to anyone on the open market.

**Open Architecture** A design which allows and encourages third party vendors to manufacture add-on products which can enhance the original design.

**Operating System** See Disk Operating System.

**OS/2** (Operating System/2) The new operating system written by Microsoft for the 286 based computers.

**Output**  Data that is sent from the computer to any device such as a printer, mouse, drive, or monitor.

**Parity**  The state of being odd or even with binary digits.  Used as an error detection technique with memory as well as with telecommunications transmissions.

**Parity Error**  This error occurs in a RAM check when the computed parity check does not agree with the parity bit.

**Parallel Port**  This port is usually found on the back of the computer and is used to transmit data eight bits at a time usually to such devices as printers.

**Peripherals**  Devices not critical to the operation of the computer but which are connected externally,  such as a printer, mouse, plotter, etc.

**Pixel**  Short for picture element.  A single dot on the screen.

**Plotter**  A type of graphics printer which uses pens to produce its output.  Used mainly for high quality graphics output.

**Port**  A connector, usually in the back of the computer, through which data enters or exits.  The typical types of ports are serial, parallel, game, and keyboard for connecting such devices as modems, printers, joy sticks, and keyboards respectively.

**Power Supply**  A device which converts AC house current into suitable DC voltages for all the electronic parts of the computer.

**Print Spooler**  A program which sets aside a portion of memory area to hold data to be printed.  This frees up the computer for other applications while information is being printed.

**Program**  A specific set of instructions which execute a task in the computer, ie. a word processing program, database program, etc.

**Prompt**  A question posed by a program.  The A:>  (A prompt) and B:> (B prompt) symbols which are used in MS-DOS are examples of prompts.

**RAM**  See Random Access Memory.

**RAM Drive**  A program which sets aside a portion of memory to act as an additional drive.  The reading and writing of information on a RAM drive can be performed about 10 times faster than on a floppy drive.

**Random Access Memory (RAM)**  Consists of chips which hold data. This data is lost when the computer is turned off.

**Read Only Memory (ROM)**  A type of chip into which a program has been permanently written.

**Resolution**  The number of points per inch on the computer screen.  The more points the better the resolution and the sharper the image.

**RGB monitor**  Stands for Red Green Blue and is a monitor for color output.

**RS 232**  See serial port.

**Screen**  The actual surface of the computer's monitor on which images are displayed.

**Serial communications**  Data is transferred one bit at a time as compared to 8 bits at a time for parallel communications.

**Serial Port**  A 25 or 9 pin connector usually on the back of a computer. Used to interface to a modem, mouse, plotter, etc.

**Software**  The non-hardware or physical part of the computer and the collective name for all programs, routines, and languages.

**Spreadsheet Program**  A calculator program using rows and columns in a grid which functions like the traditional spreadsheet.  Visicalc was the originator of the electronic spreadsheet.  Today Lotus 1-2-3 is the most popular program in this field.

**Subassembly**  A part designed to be fitted to a larger unit.  The part is already preassembled and only needs to be connected to the main unit with screws or connectors.

**Syntax**   Rules or terms used to tell the computer what function to perform.

**System Unit**  The part of the computer consisting of a chassis that contains the motherboard, power supply, drives and expansion cards.

**Throughput**  The amount of work which a computer can do in a certain amount of time.

**Turbo**  When the computer has two speeds, the higher speed is often called "turbo."  XT motherboards operating at 8 MHz or higher are referred to as turbo boards.

**Unix**  An operating system initially developed by Bell Labs for mini and mainframe computers. It has multiuser and multitasking abilities.

**User Friendly**  A term which is supposed to mean that a computer or piece of software is easy to use.

**User Group**  An association of computer users formed for the purpose of sharing information on personal computers.

**Virtual 8086 Machines**  Independently operating windows in a 386-based computer in which DOS and application software is loaded.

**Virtual Memory**  A system whereby the computer automatically swaps the contents of memory to disk storage.  In other words, it is memory which is addressable beyond the actual physical memory.  This process allows programs larger than the available memory to be operated.

**VLSI  (Very Large Scale Integration)**  A technology which allows very high density circuitry to be manufactured.

**Wait States**  A process for inserting a waiting state between the CPU and the memory, thus allowing slower memory chips to be used. Wait states are also placed on the expansion slots to allow slower expansion cards to work with today's superfast motherboards.

**Winchester Drive**  See hard drive.

**Word processing**  A program designed for the manipulation of text.

**Xenix**  A variation of the Unix operating system written by Microsoft.

**Zero Wait State**  The process of accessing memory or expansion cards at the same speed as the CPU clock.  The advantage is a net speed gain of 30 % between zero and one wait state.

# Index

# Notes

# Notes

# PC CLONE USER GROUP

**P.O. Box 15000/324, San Francisco, CA 94115**

**(415) 861-9321**

Some of the PC Clone User Group members


The PC Clone User Group is an organization whose purpose is to share information about PC Clone computers through a variety of services to the membership. The User Group is not limited to owners of any particular brand of PC clone.

## MEMBERSHIP BENEFITS & SERVICES

- Subscription to the PC Clone News; a monthly publication dedicated to current events, news and accurate information on the industry.
- Starter Disk; two useful tutorials for the beginner and experianced user.
- Tips on hardware, buying, utilities, software as well as the latest computer technology are all covered in a timely manner.
- Access to the electronic bulletin board service BBS (415) 552-9070 at 1200,N,8,1 open 24 hours.
- Monthly Membership Meeting. This takes place on the second Monday of the month at Fort Mason, Building E, Room 287, San Francisco, CA. Each meeting focuses on a special product or service followed by a "random access" (Question and Answer) session. Fee for Non-Members $2.00.

## HOW TO BECOME A MEMBER

Annual membership dues: Individuals $25, Family $30. Payable by check to PC Clone User Group, P.O. Box 15000/324, San Francisco, CA 94115. (415) 861-9321.

**Foreign memberships**

For memberships outside the continental U.S. add $12 for 1st class air mail.

**Renewals**

You will receive a renewal form in your last edition of the PC Clone News.

### PC CLONE USER GROUP
### P.O. Box 15000/324, San Francisco, CA 94115
### (415) 861-9321

Name _____ Company _____

Address _____

City _____ State _____ Zip _____

Phone _(_____)_____ Date _____

Topics of interest? _____

**Office Use Only: Mem Number: _____ Exp Date___/___/___ Amt Paid $__**

**d/n/dbf**

# IBM AT Clone Buyer's Guide and Handbook

## By Edwin Rutsch

This comprehensive and up-to-date book contains over 400 pages and is both a buying guide and a computer owners reference with an easy to follow "do-it-yourself" format. In a "reader friendly" style, it covers computers in the **$800 to $2000 price range** which can be used for **CAD, OS/2,** desktop publishing, **large spreadsheet, large database,** and **graphic intensive** applications.

## The Buyer's Guide Section Offers:

- Explanations of important computer terms and trends
- Hints, warnings, and recommendations on how to buy a low cost quality computer and expansion products
- Reviews of major AT/286 computers, including evaluations of IBM's Personal System/2 Models 50 & 60

## The Handbook Reference Section Offers:

- Instructions for upgrading an XT to a true AT/286 computer
- Money Saving Tips on how to expand the computer by adding:

    3 1/2 inch floppy drives, a hard disk, memory, improved BIOS, 80287 math coprocessor, better graphics, enhanced keyboard, modem, and more!...

- Illustrated instructions for assembling an AT clone
- Easy to understand computer troubleshooting and repair instructions

**$24.95**  plus $3.50 shipping, CA. res. add 6.5% sales tax
**Modular Information Systems, 431 Ashbury St., S F, CA 94117**

# IBM XT CLONE
# Buyer's Guide And Handbook

## By Edwin Rutsch

### Updated, Expanded, and Revised

This book is both a buying guide and a "do-it-yourself" owners reference manual. It covers computers in the **$350 to $1000 price range**, which can be used for **word processing, telecommunications, spreadsheet, database**, etc. applications.

## The Buyer's Guide Section Offers:

- Reviews of major brand name XT clones as well as the IBM Personal System/2 Models 25 and 30.

- Explanations of important computer terms and trends

- Information on how to buy a XT clone so that it can be easily upgraded and will not be obsolete tomorrow

## The Handbook Reference Section Offers:

- Money Saving Tips on how to expand the computer by adding:

  3 1/2 inch floppy drives, a hard disk, memory, improved BIOS, 8087 math coprocessor, V-20 chip, better graphics, enhanced keyboard, modem, and more!....

- Illustrated instructions for assembling an XT clone

- Easy-to-understand computer troubleshooting and repair instructions

$19.95 plus $3.50 shipping, CA. res. add 6.5% sales tax
**Modular Information Systems, 431 Ashbury St., S F, CA 94117**

# 386 COMPUTER Buyer's Guide And Handbook

### By Edwin Rutsch

This book is over 450 pages and is both a buying guide and a "do-it-yourself" owners reference source. It covers computers in the **$2000 to $6000 price range,** which can be used for **networking, CAD, graphic intensive programs, heavy number crunching, programming,** and **multitasking** applications.

## The Buyer's Guide Section Offers:

- Explanations of important computer terms and trends
- Hints, warnings, and recommendations on how to buy the computer system
- Reviews of major brand name 386-based computers, including IBM's Personal System/2 Models 70 and 80

## The Handbook Reference Section Offers:

- Complete illustrated instructions for upgrading an IBM XT and AT type computer to a true 386-based computer
- Money Saving Tips on how to expand your 386 by adding:

    3 1/2 inch floppy drives, a hard disk, memory, improved BIOS, 80387 math coprocessor, better graphics, enhanced keyboard, modem, and more!....

- Illustrated instructions for assembling a 386-based computer
- Computer troubleshooting and repair instructions

**$29.95** plus $3.50 shipping, CA. res. add 6.5% sales tax
**Modular Information Systems 431 Ashbury St., SF, CA 94117**

## Modular Information Systems
## Publishing and Composition Services

Do you need flyers, brochures, dissertations, newsletters, manuals, or books produced?  We do quality design, layout, and typesetting of your project.  This book is an example of our work!

Call or write for a free estimate:

**Modular Information Systems**
**Desktop Publishing Services**
**431 Ashbury St.**
**San Francisco, CA 94117**
**(415) 552-8648**

---

## Ventura Tips and Tricks

### By Ted Nace

The **IBM XT CLONE BUYER'S GUIDE AND HANDBOOK** was designed and typeset using Ventura Desktop Publisher.  **Ventura Tips and Tricks**, by Ted Nace, gives you a unique guide to Xerox Ventura Publisher which makes desktop publishing a reality on the 8088, 286, and 386-based computers.  This book offers: step-by-step techniques for formatting books, manuals, newsletters, forms, brochures, and business reports; precautions for using Ventura intensively without clogging your hard drive;  hidden commands and shortcuts for more efficient document formatting; notes on choosing laser printers and large-screen monitors; and an introduction to utilities for enhancing Ventura, such as HotShot, The Missing Link, and Electric Webster.

# Book Order Form

| Quantity | Description | Unit Price | Amount |
|---|---|---|---|
| | **NEW!** IBM XT Clone Buyer's Guide and Handbook | 19.95 | |
| | IBM AT Clone Buyer's Guide and Handbook | 24.95 | |
| | 386 Computer Buyer's Guide and Handbook | 29.95 | |
| | Ventura Tips and Tricks | 18.95 | |
| | | | |
| | | | |

CA res. add 6.5% sales tax (XT-$.65, AT-$1.62, 386-$1.94, Ven-$1.23)
U.S. shipping: $3.50 first item, $1 each additional item
Canadian shipping: $5 first item, $2 each additional item
Overseas shipping: $10 fist item, $3 each additional item

Dealers, user groups, distributors, volume purchasers;  write for
volume discount schedual.

| | |
|---|---|
| **Subtotal** | |
| **Tax** | |
| **Shipping** | |
| **Total** | |
| | |

Name _____

Address _____

City _____ State _____ Zip _____

Mail  check or money order to:

**Modular Information Systems**
**431 Ashbury St.**
**San Francisco, CA 94117**

# *Feedback Form*

This book is continuously being updated, expanded, and revised. It is very help-ful to recieve feedback from readers in order to improve it. Please take some time and let me know what you think. Thanks.

Is there any other information you would like to see in this book or any correc-tions? Was any wording unclear or ambiguous? If so where?

What other products do you think should be mentioned in this book?

What was your overall impression of this buyer's guide and handbook?

May your comments be used as promotional material?

❐ Yes
❐ No

Name:

# Public Domain Software

Public Domain Software is similar to public domain books and photographs. It has no copyright protection and may be freely copied and shared for any purpose. Some of these packages are quite complex and extensive. The advantage for the buyer of this software is that you can copy it as many times as necessary for as many machines as necessary in order to standardize your office or place of business without the need for site licensing or the purchase of additional packages.

It's also usually no more than $10 or so a disk. If it doesn't do what you want, you can always use the disk as a coffee coaster or something.

# Shareware

In the blizzard of expensive full color glossy software advertisements, shareware is probably one of the biggest secrets in software today.

Shareware is a different concept in software sales. The main idea behind it is "try before you buy". The software can be freely copied and distributed, *but . . . if you use it you are expected to register and pay the author for your copy. We strongly urge you to do this and help keep software costs low.*

Usually registering gets you a typeset manual, upgrades, and phone support (!). Generally (though not always), these packages are more extensive, complex and useful than public domain software. Many, like PC-Write and PC-File are as good as or superior to other commercial packages.

It's usually a lot cheaper than most other commercial software. Registration cost to get manuals and support is about one-fourth to one-tenth of the cost. To acquire the working programs from us for testing costs six dollars per disk. So if it doesn't do what you want or you never use it, you're not out $350. And if you compare the **price-performance-ratio** with most commercial packages, you will see what a real value it is. Remember though, the fee we charge is only for the copying and distribution of the software. It does not include support. For support you must become a registered user with the author of the software package.

# Software and Integration Packages

On the following pages are a list of the most useful public domain and shareware packages we could find. In addition we have developed packages for both beginning and experienced users at a reduced price.

We offer three packages: the **Commercial-Compatibility Package**, the **Super-User-Friendly Package**, and the **Starter Package**.

The first two packages include a Word Processor, Database, Spreadsheet and Disk Manager all tied together with asingle keystroke menues.

The third is a collection of useful programs and utilities for the beginning computer user.

## THE COMPATIBILITY PACKAGE*

This is for the user that needs Lotus and dBase compatibilty. They also represent some the most versatile and advanced shareware on the market today. These programs are easily as good or better than other commercial software.

**AS EASY AS** - The Lotus compatible spreadsheet, allows use of Lotus files. It works and acts like Lotus with some limitations.
**WAMPUM (2 disks)** - The menu driven dBase clone. Uses and creates dBase compatible files.
**PC-WRITE (2 disks)** - A truly full featured word processor, easily as good as or better than most commercial word processing software. It contains mailmerge, spellcheck, etc.
**STILL RIVER SHELL** - Gives you a visual "picture" of files and directories on your hard disk. Performs almost all of the functions of DOS such as copying and deleting of files, but allows you to see what you're doing.

## THE SUPER-USER-FRIENDLY PACKAGE*

While the programs in the compatibility package will do almost anything the commercial programs will do, some of them are almost as difficult to use as commercial software. The Super-User-Friendly Package solves that problem. These packages were chosen for their many features *and* ease of use. They contain:

**EZ-SPREADSHEET** - Easy to use but powerful spreadsheet for the first time user.
**NEW YORK WORD  (2 disks)** - The user friendly word processor
**FILE EXPRESS (2 disks)** - Menu driven database. Quite good. Quite powerful.
**STILL RIVER SHELL** - Gives you a visual "picture" of files and directories on your hard disk. Performs almost all of the functions of DOS such as copying and deleting of files, but allows you to see what you're doing.

* As time goes by, we find better software for these packages, so we reserve the right to substitute any of the programs in these packages with something comparable or better at anytime and without notice.

## STARTER PACKAGE

This is a collection of 12 useful disks full of software programs which is especially good for the new computer user.  These disks are; **Computer Tutor, DOS Help, DOS Tips, Troubleshooting, Clone Tester, Deskmate, Menuing DOS Shells, General Utilities #1, General Utilities #2, Printer Utilities,** and **Keyboard Utilities.**

# *Software Order Form*

## BUSINESS
- ☐ **EZ-Forms** - business form generation, completion, and printing program.
- ☐ **Letters** - 100, fill in the blanks, time saving business letters.
- ☐ **Lable Maker** - program for making lables.

## DATABASES
- ☐ **PC-File** (2 disks)* - well known and popular database program.
- ☐ **PC-Graph** - create graphics directly from PC-File.
- ☐ **File Express** (2 disks)* - menu driven database for info. mgt., mailing labels, etc.
- ☐ **Wampum** - menu driven shareware clone of the popular dBase III program.
- ☐ **Newbase** - user-friendly menu driven database system.

## EDUCATION AND COMPUTER TUTORING
- ☐ **Computer Tutor** - learn about the computer.
- ☐ **DOS Help** - immediate reference to DOS commands.
- ☐ **DOS Tips** (2 disks)* - advanced DOS tutorial.
- ☐ **PC Type** - (3 disks)* practice touch typing.
- ☐ **Batch Tutor** - learn how to set up and use batch files.
- ☐ **Lotus 1-2-3 Tutor** - for beginners, requires Lotus 1-2-3.

## FINANCE
- ☐ **Time and Money** - easy to use record keeping program.
- ☐ **Checkbook** - convenient and simple management of banking records.
- ☐ **Checkpro** - easy checking, savings, credit card management.
- ☐ **CPA Ledger** (3 disks)* - a complete general ledger.
- ☐ **PC Accountant** (2 disks)* - a complete personal bookkeeping system.
- ☐ **PC payroll** - menu driven payroll system.
- ☐ **Mr. Bill** (2 disks)* - For billing customers, client reports, invoices, audit trail.
- ☐ **PC Stock** - analyze market trends, includes graphics.
- ☐ **APF** - project scheduler with up to 17 variables.

## GRAPHICS
- ☐ **PC-Key-Draw** - mouseless drawing program for the PC. (CGA req'd)
- ☐ **Dancad3d** (4 disks)* - 3-D CAD for architects and engineers. Includes advanced slide and animation capabilities similar to commercial CAD. (CGA req'd)
- ☐ **CAD and Supergraph** - another CAD program. (CGA req'd)
- ☐ **Altmira Editor** - create graphs, charts, logos, pictures. (CGA req'd)

## GAMES
- ☐ **Mono Graphics #1** - Star Wars, Rlogic, Blackjack, Gomuku, more!
- ☐ **Mono Graphics #2** - Pac-gal, Air Traffic Controller, Trek Run, more!
- ☐ **Color Graphics #1** - Sopwith, Pango, Space War, Pin Ball, more!
- ☐ **Color Graphics #2** - Twilight Zone, JumpJoe, Flightmare, more!
- ☐ **Color Graphics #3** - Fighter, Digger, Bouncing Babies, 3-Demon, more!
- ☐ **Color Graphics #4** - Draw Poker, Cuizo, Hopper, more!
- ☐ **BASIC Color Games** – games written in BASIC language.
- ☐ **Flight Simulator** – somewhat like the commercial version.
- ☐ **EGA Games** - EGA Risk, Roids, Breakout, plus demos.

## MUSIC AND SOUNDS
- ☐ **PC Musician** - music composition and playing.
- ☐ **Music and Sounds** - wide variety of sounds and a speech demo.

## PROGRAMMING

- ☐ **Logo** - teaches simple programming to children.
- ☐ **Basic tutor** - interactive Basic programming tutorial.
- ☐ **Basic Aids and Routines** - makes BASIC programming easier.
- ☐ **Turbo pascal tutor** - lessons on Turbo Pascal.
- ☐ **Turbo Aids and Routines** (4 disks)* - makes Pascal programming easier.
- ☐ **C language -** small C compiler and interpreter.
- ☐ **C Aids and Routines** (4 disks)* - makes C programming easier.

## SPREADSHEETS

- ☐ **PC-Calc** - spreadsheet program similar to Lotus 1-2-3.
- ☐ **AS EASY AS** - another Lotus like spreadsheet.
- ☐ **EZ SPREADSHEET** - easy-to-use menu driven spreadsheet.

## TELECOMMUNICATIONS

- ☐ **Qmodem** - A telecommunications program with features that automate dialing.

## TROUBLESHOOTING

- ☐ **Troubleshooting** - (menu driven) check for RAM errors, checks ports, parts list, hard disk diagnostics and analysis, and more.

## UTILITIES

- ☐ **Clone Tester** - test the computer and hard drive speed, IBM BIOS compat., etc.
- ☐ **Deskmate** - the shareware version of the popular program, Sidekick. Contains mini-word processor, typewriter, calculator, modem dialer, and more.
- ☐ **Menuing DOS shells** - a collection of DOS shells, choose the one you like the best.
- ☐ **General Utilities #1** - slow down the computer, and many other invaluable utilities.
- ☐ **General Utilities #2** - more of the most useful DOS utilities.
- ☐ **Printer** - print spooler, sideways printing, banner makers, more!
- ☐ **Hard Disk -** utilities to control your hard disk.
- ☐ **Keyboard** - utilities to make your keyboard more versatile and efficient.
- ☐ **Encryption and security** - protect sensitive information with these programs.

## WORD PROCESSING

- ☐ **PC -Write** (2 disks)* - a truly FULL FEATURED word processor.
- ☐ **New York Word** - (2 disks)* - easy yet powerful word processor.
- ☐ **PC-Outline -** thought organizing and outlining program.
- ☐ **PC-Style** - analyze your writing style.

---

| | | |
|---|---|---|
| * All prices are per disk | | |
| Please send disks checked above # _____ | X  $6 per disk | _____ |
| Compatibility Package | $39 | _____ |
| Super-User-Friendly Package | $39 | _____ |
| Starter Pack (12 disks) | $59 | _____ |
| California residents add 6.5% sales tax | | _____ |
| +$4 per order (shipping and handling) | | _____ |
| Enclosed is a check or money order for Total | | _____ |

Name _____

Address_____

City _____ State_____ Zip _____

Mail to: **Modular Information Systems,  431 Ashbury St., San Francisco, Ca 94117**